# STUDENT POLITICS AND
# HIGHER EDUCATION

# STUDENT POLITICS
# AND
# HIGHER EDUCATION

*by*
*Digby Jacks*

1975
LAWRENCE AND WISHART
LONDON

© Digby Jacks 1975

SBN: 85315 326 4 (hardback)
SBN: 85315 328 0 (paperback)

*Printed in Great Britain by*
*The Camelot Press Ltd, Southampton*

To Sonia and Matthew

# ACKNOWLEDGEMENTS

It is impossible to write a book without the assistance of many people. The hundreds of people I worked with before and during the time I was an officer of the NUS have been unknowing assistants. I have been particularly glad to consult a number of current officers of the National Union of Students—Steve Parry, Al Stewart and Charles Clarke. Invaluable assistance has been obtained from a number of NUS staff, notably Neville Ealden, its Finance Secretary, Stella Greenall, for many years an unrivalled expert on student grants and a wide variety of educational questions, and Edward Garraty, a linchpin in the Union's grasp of legal and constitutional matters. All commented constructively and critically on what I had to say; the loyalty of long-serving members of NUS staff is a central feature of the organisation's strength.

A number of comrades and friends have provided me with invaluable political criticism. Former colleagues in the Union—Leo Smith, Jeff Staniforth, Dave Wynn and Phil Goodwin have been particularly helpful. Likewise Fergus Nicholson, Dave Cook and Jon Bloomfield, successive National Student Organisers of the Communist Party, have guided and assisted me. Much is owed Fergus Nicholson for years of patient and principled work in the cause of a mass and militant student movement. Colin Sweet who occupied the same position in the mid-1950's helped on a number of historical aspects. Dave Pavitt, Jack Woddis and Lothar Letsche helped me on some international points; while Neil Vann gave me some useful information about the role of the Labour Party in student affairs.

Writing this book has proved to be both an arduous and enjoyable activity. Without the assistance of both David Gilles and Maurice Cornforth the structure of the book would have been quite inadequate. Finally, I must express my gratitude to Hilda Jacks who willingly undertook the task of typing the manuscript.

D. J.

# CONTENTS

Introduction 9

1. Higher Education: Conservatism and change 14
   The Robbins Report
   An assessment of Robbins
   Social class and higher education
   Women and post-school education
   The binary system
   Non-advanced further education
   Polytechnics
   Colleges of education
   The art colleges
   The universities
   The influence of business and industry
   The 1972 White Paper and the future

2. The Circumstances of Students 53
   Student finance
   Student housing
   Student counselling and graduate unemployment
   Student representation
   Student discipline
   Student assessment
   General educational matters

3. The Development of Student Unions and the National Union
   of Students 73
   Origins
   The National Union of Students

4. The Student Movement, 1966–74 86

5. The Character of the Student Movement 97
   Students and the working class
   The Communist Party of Great Britain
   The Labour Party

The vanguard
Red bases
The Conservative Party

6. Perspectives and Policies     118
    Educational issues
      Student financing
      Assessment and teaching methods
      Access and entry qualifications
      The government of colleges and universities
      The curriculum and the objectives of education
      The comprehensive framework
    Student Organisations and the Student Movement

Appendices     161
1. A Charter of Student Rights and Responsibilities, 1940     161
2. A Radical Student Alliance, 1966     163
3. RSSF—Manifesto for a Political Programme, 1968     165
4. The Nature of Student Unions     167

    Index     171

# INTRODUCTION

Ten years ago Ferdynand Zweig wrote of a survey of student opinion at Oxford and Manchester Universities: "The model student should be interested in politics, but should not take up politics. He searches and examines the records of political parties and other movements, and tries to separate the wheat from the chaff, but he is largely disillusioned with parties, often regarding politics as a dirty and dishonourable business. . . . He should remember that all great achievements of British political history were due primarily to the British genius for compromise" (*The Student in an Age of Anxiety*, Heinemann 1963, pp. 194, 196). Whilst it would be naïve to say that no students continue to hold these views, the norm has changed. This book will examine why. It is intended for the interested general reader, all those concerned with higher and further education, and particularly the student activist. It seeks to document and assess the origins and development of the student movement in Britain and to consider critically various perspectives that have been argued. The changes that have taken place in the student world have been remarkable and of considerable political significance. The student body, organised and active, is now a force for social progress. Such a statement ten years ago would have been regarded as wishful thinking.

The book is broadly divided into three parts. The first two chapters deal with the background—the development of further and higher education and the circumstances that students find themselves in. Chapters 3 and 4 cover the history of student organisations and the student movement in Britain. Finally, the last two attempt an analysis of the character of the movement and my views on future perspectives.

I hope that what I have written will assist an understanding of student affairs. Misconceptions and prejudices about students abound—that they are a pampered élite, that they are all iconoclasts, that they are petty bourgeois and will all end up as respectable Tory voting fodder. Public attitudes have not yet caught up with the reality of the expansion of higher and further education that has taken place in the last ten years.

Nearly one quarter of the age-group are now in full-time post-school education. Yet students are still regarded in many quarters as the managers and well-to-do of the future.

The press has a very chequered record in dealing with students. In 1966–9 any student political activity was greeted by scare headlines, "Student Revolution", and given generally exaggerated and distorted publicity. The press sought to stigmatise students, alienate the general public from them and weaken the effect of their actions. More recently the press has come to regard what students do as irrelevant or not "newsworth", presumably because it has happened before and there's not enough violence, etc. Some journalists have been taken in by their own clichés and from time to time pronounce the student movement "dead". A sceptic might comment that this is because student campaigns and activities are generally relatively successful these days—that's not news. Nevertheless, some individual journalists, particularly successive education correspondents of the *Guardian* and Peter Wilby of the *Observer*, together with the *Morning Star*, have done much to promote an understanding of students by accurate reporting and incisive and sympathetic writing.

At the same time students have not been very effective in getting their views across, at least not until fairly recently. Adventurist tactics have played into the hands of anti-student elements in the media. In 1968 "student revolutionaries" revelled in the notoriety given them by the capitalist press and some even talked of establishing a "revolutionary presence" as a result of press publicity. In the 1970's the situation has improved somewhat. The main reason for this has been the increased authority and important strategic position occupied by the National Union of Students.

One of my concerns in writing this book is to document the developments that have taken place. To the highly committed individual concerned with immediate problems, actions and results, what happened in the previous years, the mistakes made and the experience gained, may seem quite irrelevant. Any movement seeking change must appreciate that there are many lessons to be learned from the past. Yet there is an unfortunate historical and even antihistorical attitude amongst many student leaders and activists. This is accentuated by the rapid turnover in the student population, for whom what happened more than three or four years ago is passed on as a vague folk-lore. The history of the student movement, student unions and the NUS is inadequately documented. I hope this book is a contribution towards remedying this.

What of the books that have been written in recent years? In my view there is a marked dearth of substantial material. Much is emphemeral and does not stand the test of time. For the NUS there is a shortage of source material covering the full span of the Union's history. Frank Rhodes (1966–7) has written a useful and detailed thesis on the development of the Union's organisation, which I have been pleased to draw on. Eric Ashby and Mary Anderson in their book *The Rise of the Student Estate* (1969) have written the only extant substantial volume. It contains much material of value but suffers from an eclecticism and diffuseness making it difficult to read. The title "estate" is unfortunate, the book is written from the point of view of the liberal university establishment and has been characterised as Whig history. The authors are critical of militant student unionism and regard the acme of development of the "estate" as the 1968 NUS-VCC-AEC joint statements. Both of these held back progress in the field of student representation at the time.

Perhaps the best book that has been written to date, and certainly the least pretentious, is the LSE Research Monograph *Students in Conflict* (1970) by Tessa Blackstone, Kathleen Gales, Roger Hadley and Wyn Lewis. This assembles a large amount of research material about student attitudes and seeks to assess them in an objective manner. To my knowledge this is the only research material on student voting inclinations that has recently been published. It is certainly much more useful than the spate of quasi-memoirs that successive LSE disputes produced from the administration: Sir Sydney Caine, *British Universities—Purposes and Prospects*, Bodley Head 1969, and Harry Kidd, *The Trouble at LSE,* Oxford 1969; and from a student direction Colin Crouch, *The Student Revolt*, Bodley Head 1969, and Paul Hoch, *LSE The Natives are Restless*, Sheed and Ward 1969.

The experiences of the 1968 events in France generated a number of books. Penguin published Cohn-Bendit's rambling and self-indulgent *Obsolete Communism—The Left-Wing Alternative*; Panther a series of interviews in adulation of the figures deemed by the press, particularly *Le Monde*, to be at the nerve centre of "Les événements"—*The Student Revolt*. Panther also published the semi-poetical *The Beginning of the*

*End* by Angelo Quattrocchi and Tom Nairn, a rather dated eulogy to student vanguardism. Perhaps the best book in English on France at this time is John Gretton's *Students and Workers* (Macdonald 1969). There is no substitute for reading the untranslated and substantial French works on this matter. Penguin in 1969 also published *Student Power*. This contains a number of essays of particular interest to those concerned with 1968. Penguin Education paperbacks have produced a number of very useful little books over the last five years: *The Impact of Robbins* by Layard and King, *Patterns and Policies in Higher Education* by Charles Carter *et al.*; *Teaching and Learning in Higher Education* by Ruth Beard, *The Hornsey Affair* by students and staff of the Hornsey College of Art and *Warwick University Ltd* by E. P. Thompson and others.

Two books require particular mention: *The Student Revolt* by Colin Crouch (The Bodley Head 1969) and *Student Power*, ed. Julian Nagel (Merlin 1969). Crouch concentrates almost entirely on the developments at the LSE, from his own particular slant. He completely underestimates everything that took place elsewhere, and in the art colleges in particular in 1968. He accepts the binary policy for higher education. He does, however, have a number of interesting observations to make about the Labour Party and the student movement. Nagel's book is a collection of articles about student movements in a number of countries. It concludes with a "grand" essay entitled "World Cultural Revolution?" Like the Penguin book of the same title it enters into the spirit of the time, the fashionable theme of the student as the "detonator" of the revolution. This notion and the events of 1968 generally are given a close scrutiny in what follows. On the general question of academic freedom which impinges on the development of the student movement Anthony Arblaster's *Academic Freedom* (Penguin 1974) is a valuable contribution. The thorny questions of freedom of speech and academic freedom are lucidly and adequately dealt with as far as student activities are concerned in his chapter 7. Yet some of his more general statements about student affairs have a libertarian and anarchistic flavour with which I cannot agree. In particular, seeking the origins of student radicalism he avers: "Students will continue to enjoy a sense of being abnormally free from the constraints of society and the economy. It is this more than anything else that explains the phenomenon of student radicalism." Levels of grant, housing, conditions generally and job opportunities clearly contradict this. More particularly, this statement distinguishes not at all present-day students from those pre-Robbins or their aristocratic precursors.

Several words and phrases which recur throughout the present book need some clarification at the outset. The words "Union", "NUS" and "National Union of Students" are interchangeable. The term "student movement" has been widely used. It is difficult to define, but I have always found the following description best: "The sum total of actions and intentions of students individually, collectively and organisationally that are directed for change in the students' own circumstances and for educational and wider social change." It is not the same term as "student body", which means all those who are students at a given time, all those registered on courses, members of student unions, etc. Likewise, on a point of definition, the NUS is not the same as the NUS Executive, as some seem to think. It is the voluntary federation of the overwhelming majority of student unions in Britain, giving corporate and political expression to the student body at a national level.

To the reader two things will soon become obvious—the involvement of the author and his partisan viewpoint. The book is written from a personal slant which seeks, among other things, to expound the Communist stance on the student movement. I make no apology for tendentious writing as I believe an objective understanding of events is aided by participation. Strongly held views can be more illuminating than pseudo-scientific objectivity and mere banal description. Certainly, no one who ignores contentious views, seeks to limit the influence of ideological matters or derides political commitment can reach any very satisfactory assessment of the student movement in recent times. But I have not written a book which is primarily one of Marxist theory or one essentially concerned with education. In any attempt to present a balanced view of the growth and potential of the student movement, ideology, theory, politics and education are all inextricably mixed.

I write with the hope that the mass of students can be permanently won to the side of the working class. This process has begun. It must be concluded.

D. J.

# 1

## HIGHER AND FURTHER EDUCATION:
## CONSERVATISM AND CHANGE

To understand the contemporary student movement it is necessary to see how Government policy has changed, how the institutions of higher and further education have developed and how their broader social and economic role has altered. This is an essential preliminary to looking at the students' immediate circumstances, grievances and attitudes. Some have tried to analyse and project a strategy based on the unstated assumption that students act entirely on the basis of a sort of "free will", unrelated to the situations in which they find themselves. Equally fallacious is the view that students should be understood purely in political terms, as though they were all "100 per cent political animals". The primary point of reference for the student, both objectively and subjectively, is the college or university. It is this which gives him his identity and in it he seeks to pursue a course of education and other related activities. But students, like everyone else, do not simply react to pressures applied to them, and the development of the student movement is not merely a function of developments within the educational system.

This chapter will set out the main changes that have taken place in the colleges and universities over the last decade. The account will not be very detailed or claim to be definitive on every point. Its purpose is to sketch in a backcloth. Policies and attitudes developed by the NUS and students unions will also be alluded to. It is an assessment as well as a description. It will start with the Robbins Report, then consider the system as a whole before looking at each sector in some detail, and finishing with the 1972 White Paper and the future prospects.

### The Robbins Report

On February 8th, 1961, the Robbins Committee was established by Treasury minute. Two and a half years later it reported to the Prime Minister (October 1963). Twenty-four hours after the report appeared the Government published its own White Paper which accepted the

Committee's major quantitative recommendations, and action on this White Paper soon followed. The fabric of further and higher education was to change rapidly in the next decade: student numbers doubled, many new institutions were established and older ones reformed. The quantitative aspects of the Report were relatively well researched and, unlike other educational reports, it went direct to the Prime Minister. Its central recommendations were not lost in the corridors of the Department of Education and Science. Such was its status and importance at the time.

Why the urgency for action? Throughout the 1950's it became increasingly apparent to the Tory Government and big business that Britain's economic position was becoming increasingly less competitive. Britain was ceasing to be a world power and a major imperialist nation. They thought that technological and scientific progress might provide an answer. Britain did not compare well with the United States, the Soviet Union (especially after Sputnik I in 1957) and many other countries in the output of skilled scientists and technologists.

This was doubly bad for Britain, for the dependence on imports and the deficiency in natural resources rendered her best resource—her skills and brains—even more important than in other countries. Put another way, technological progress within the productive relations of capitalism required a more highly skilled and specialised and, incidentally, a better educated work force. Higher education, and the universities in particular, were seen as the institutions capable of producing the manpower Britain needed.

Other subsidiary factors were important, though the Committee in its report skilfully gave them equal status with the economic arguments. After the Second World War there was a substantial and short-term increase in the birth-rate. This produced an educational "bulge", an increase in school population ascending the school system in the 1950's. In 1959 there was 579,000 eighteen-year-olds. In 1965 there were 881,000. Associated with this was a marked increase (or "trend") in educational achievement as measured by the possession of formal school-leaving qualifications. This resulted in a rapid increase in social demand for higher and further education at the end of the 1950's. Like the eleven-plus and the position of grammar school places in the mid 1950's, university entrance became an important political issue. Both the Report and the Tory Government found it desirable to meet, or rather assuage, this demand. This was particularly expedient in view of the impending 1964 general election. The Report also saw education as a social good, and accordingly expansion as a desirable objective. The frontiers of knowledge needed extension and "common standards of citizenship" required development.

The educational principle asserted was that "courses of higher education should be available for all those who are qualified by ability and attainment to pursue them and who wish to do so". This requires some elucidation, for at the time some saw it as a hideous dilution of the academic excellence of the universities—the admission of the educational "great unwashed". *The Times* and the rest of the "more means worse" brigade seem still to hold this view. In fact it meant entry to anyone who had two "A" levels (established as the normal minimum university entrance requirement in 1953), or their academic equivalent—and who wanted a higher education. This by any account is restrictive, especially when not all those with two "A" levels secure entry. Perhaps what the opponents at the time objected to most was rejection of the "limited pool of ability" concept. In line with the economic requirements of the time it was concerned to utilise fully the available abilities within the population:

"But we believe it is highly misleading to suppose that one can determine an upper limit to the number of people who could benefit from higher education, given favourable circumstances. . . . It is no doubt true that there are a born number of potential 'firsts' whose qualities are such that they win through whatever their environmental disadvantages, and another considerably larger number, who, if trained by the most famous teachers in history, would still fail their examinations. But in between there is a vast mass whose performance, both at the entry to higher education and beyond, depends greatly on how they have lived and been taught beforehand . . . the belief that there exists some easy method of ascertaining an intelligence factor unaffected by education or background is outmoded."

Basing itself on the number of well-qualified school-leavers that were projected for the future the Report recommended a crash programme of expansion for higher education. There were to be 390,000 full-time places in higher education by 1973–4 and 560,000 in 1981. In order to accommodate this rapid increase in student numbers the existing universities and colleges were expanded, a number of new universities developed very fast and the Colleges of Advanced Technology were elevated to university status.

Robbins placed a high premium on scientific research and recommended the establishment of five Special Institutions for Scientific and Technological Education and Research (SISTER's). Finally, the report recommended that the proportion of students in universities, as compared with other institutions of higher and further education, should increase from 55 per cent—the 1962 proportion—to 60 per cent in 1980.

## An assessment of Robbins

There can be no doubt that the Robbins Report and the decisions taken in consequence of it have irrevocably altered the higher education system, the development of which must be seen as one of the most important aspects of the social history of the 1960's. Larger quantities of skilled manpower have been put at the disposal of the British economy. What has been the effect? It has not solved the economic problems as the architects and sponsors of the Report had hoped. In particular, the Wilsonian euphoria about "the white heat of the technological revolution" has not forged a better and richer Britain—so far as the majority of people are concerned. Indeed, the graduate unemployment or under-employment that has appeared in recent years might to some indicate that there was no point in the expenditure at all. At the cynical level it could be replied that given the importance of state expenditure in maintaining capitalist economy, higher education was as good an option for the state as any other, and certainly more acceptable politically than grand imperial adventures overseas. The reason that the universities initially and the polytechnics latterly have not been able to solve Britain's economic crisis is that the causes of the malaise lie much deeper than the supply of skilled manpower. If the system itself is in crisis, if there is inadequate investment in Britain as opposed to more lucrative projects abroad, if military expenditure is at a very high and inflationary level, if the currency exists more for the benefit of international monopolies and speculators than for the British people, and finally, if governments have systematically pursued deflationary policies, dear money policies and promoted unemployment, it is hardly surprising that Britain's best brains are unable to have much effect—however well they are trained. Capitalism wastes the talents of the working people in unemployment, and in times of crisis the talents of graduates are also neglected or squandered.

The positive results of the Robbins Report must not be looked for in terms of problems it could not solve. It is rather the expansion of educational opportunity and a greater social dispersion of the results and benefits of higher education that the Robbins Report has been instrumental in creating. In other respects a more critical assessment is necessary. Robbins was primarily a report for the universities. It proposed a Ministry of Arts and Science which would be the "apex of the autonomous sector of higher education". Schools and further education would have been dealt with separately by the Minister of Education. This proposal was rejected by the Government of the day. It would have been a very élitist administrative structure, making the divisions in post-school education even sharper than they are—though the universities disliked the idea of a separate Ministry for different reasons. In general the report had very little to say about non-advanced further education and part-time education. It advocated the absorption of the teachers training colleges, renamed colleges of education, into the universities on the universities' terms as Schools of Education (a proposal which was rejected by the Government). Though it did not specifically advocate the binary system, in practice it would have differed little from the overall binary policy if all its recommendations had been implemented. In particular its view of the universities was as autonomous, élitist and privileged institutions. Underlying this was the conception of a meritocratic élite surrounded by a two "A" level entry requirement.

Governments have not sought to give universities the full status that Robbins intended. In the latter part of the 1960's the colleges of education and the polytechnics expanded at a relatively faster rate. The Labour Government in 1966 sought to build up higher education in the public sector at selected centres, the polytechnics, as an alternative to the universities. This is the binary policy variant chosen by the Department of Education and Science and adopted by all governments since.

Measured by the number of qualified school-leavers the Robbins estimates for expansion have been shown to be completely inadequate. In 1970 the Department of Education and Science estimated, in *Educational Planning Paper 2*, that in England and Wales the number of places in full-time education which would be required in 1981 to meet the demand from school-leavers with two "A" levels or their equivalent would be 727,000. If to this is added the corresponding estimate from the Scottish Education Department, the estimated requirement of places in 1981 comes to 831,000, as against the 560,000 of Robbins. The DES document estimated that by 1981 the numbers of male school-leavers with two "A" levels would be 97,000 and of females 75,000. Both these figures are nearly double the 1971 figures. The NUS, NUT and some other educational organisations think that the *Educational Planning Paper 2* figure is itself too conservative to provide the sort of higher education system that the country will need in the 1980's. The NUS in particular pointed out that the DES plans in 1970 were based on inadequate assumptions—that the numbers of mature and overseas students would not increase after 1971; that the proportion of women students in higher education would be less in 1981 than it was in 1967; that the proportion of students with the requisite number of "A" level passes *not* securing access to higher education would increase; that the proportion of students continuing to postgraduate study would decrease; that there would be no scope for the lengthening or "mix" of courses; that college of education entrant numbers would be held static; and that the rate of expansion of the system would slow down.

The Tory Government in its White Paper *Education a Framework for Expansion* said that student numbers would be 750,000 in 1981. Like the *Educational Planning Paper 2* figure it will turn out to be too low. Since then the situation has worsened and it is now certain that even this modest figure will not be met because of the Government's cuts in public expenditure in December 1973.

In 1971 it was more difficult to get to university than it was in 1961. The reason for this was the very rapid increase in the number of qualified school-leavers. By 1981, if present trends continue, it may be more difficult still. Although Robbins charted an expansionist future, its scale and all subsequent Government plans have been insufficient. At least the Robbins expansion meant the defeat of the deeply entrenched "more means worse" lobby. In 1970 the Committee of Vice-Chancellors and Principals stated: "Experience since the war has shown that, as the general educational standard of the country improves, the horizons of opportunity are widened, the proportion of young people admitted to the universities can be increased without perceptible fall in intellectual ability or awareness of those gaining entry." This is the limited but positive achievement of the Robbins Report.

## Social class and higher education

Whilst it is possible for anyone from any social background to become a student at university or college, for many this is only a theoretical right and opportunity. Access to higher and further education is disproportionately weighted in favour of the better-off sections of the population. Professor Kelsall showed that in 1955–6 only 9 per cent of those admitted to Cambridge University and 13 per cent in the case of Oxford University came from working-class sections of the population; that 75 per cent of male students at Cambridge and 60 per cent at Oxford came from public schools and direct grant grammar schools; and that respectively 27 per cent and 39 per cent of entrants has been educated at LEA maintained secondary grammar schools. For the universities as a whole in the same year only one-quarter of the students were of working-class origin—27 per cent of men and 19 per cent of women. The Robbins Report definitively outlined the extent of inequality of access:

PERCENTAGE OF CHILDREN BORN IN 1940–1
REACHING FULL-TIME HIGHER EDUCATION:
BY FATHER'S OCCUPATION IN GREAT BRITAIN

| Father's occupation | Full-time h.e. degree level | Other | No full-time h.e. | All children as % | Numbers |
|---|---|---|---|---|---|
| | BOYS AND GIRLS TOGETHER | | | | |
| Higher professional | 33 | 12 | 55 | 100 | 15,000 |
| Managerial and other professional | 11 | 8 | 81 | 100 | 87,000 |
| Clerical | 6 | 4 | 90 | 100 | 38,000 |

| Father's occupation | Full-time h.e. degree level | Other | No full-time h.e. | All children as % | Numbers |
|---|---|---|---|---|---|
| Skilled manual | 2 | 2 | 96 | 100 | 278,000 |
| Semi and unskilled manual | 1 | 1 | 98 | 100 | 189,000 |
| BOYS AND GIRLS SEPARATED | | | | | |
| Boys | | | | | |
| Non-manual | 15 | 4 | 81 | 100 | 70,000 |
| Manual | 3 | 2 | 95 | 100 | 189,000 |
| Girls | | | | | |
| Non-manual | 9 | 10 | 81 | 100 | 70,000 |
| Manual | 1 | 2 | 97 | 100 | 196,000 |

Two comments need to be made on this table. First, the position concerning women. There is a general and supplementary discrimination against the female sex gaining access to higher education. In the table above it can be seen that the daughters of manual workers have one-third the chance of entering higher education (universities) that their brothers have, and one-fifteenth the chance of boys from non-manual backgrounds. Secondly, these figures make no reference to other forms of post-school education, part-time work, evening studies, day release and non-advanced work in general. It is in this area that the majority of working-class young people who have some form of education beyond the school-leaving age are to be found.

The social inequality so sharply demonstrated by the figures above has been widely documented by the Newsom and Crowther Reports, by the Douglas Survey and, most recently, by the survey undertaken by the National Children's Bureau—*From Birth to Seven*. In this last survey it was shown that the less privileged sections of the population are between two and four years retarded at school at the age of seven in comparison to middle-class children. All these reports and surveys have starkly shown the extent of inequality within the education system at every level.

It is not my purpose here to examine in detail the reasons for this inequality—why the sons and daughters of working-class people do not obtain access to levels of educational provision commensurate with their numerical strength in the population. Evidently the reasons are complex—part economic and part social and cultural. Certainly the sons and daughters of well-to-do parents are better able to stay on at school! or enter full-time education because the parents can more easily subsidise them. These same parents, too, are likely to be ambitious in respect of their children's educational attainment. By comparison working-class young people tend to have their expectations formed by the employment and social experience of their parents. Indeed, it is an economic necessity that many earn an income as soon as they can. In addition there is the reaction of the working-class child to the school as an institution. The child from a middle-class background is better suited to doing well in this environment. The speech used, the dominant values, the construction of the curriculum and the authority system are more akin to what the middle-class child has experienced in his home. These and other factors combine to make up a social reality—working-class young people end up in broadly the same position as their parents.

It is often stated that the British system of higher education treats working-class people more favourably than the systems of comparable countries. The same claim, with greater justification, is made of the British system of student support.

Yet it is extremely difficult to secure comparable data. What one Government or official bureau of statistics regards as working-class is not the same as others. Some say that it is this difference which makes Britain appear favourably in international comparisons. It is in any case clear that the socialist countries have a higher proportion of working-class young people in all types of higher education.

How has this discriminatory and most unsatisfactory situation changed over the years? The following table from the Robbins Report gives an indication.

PERCENTAGE OF BOYS AGED 18 IN 1928–47
AND 1960 ENTERING UNIVERSITY: BY SOCIAL CLASS

| Social class | Boys aged 18 expressed as a percentage | |
| --- | --- | --- |
| | *1928–47* | *1960* |
| A. Non-manual | 8·9 | 16·8 |
| B. Manual | 1·4 | 2·6 |
| C. All boys | 3·7 | 6·5 |
| A divided by B | 6·4 | 6·5 |

It shows a boy with a "non-manual" background had 6·4 times the chance of entering university than the son of "manual" parents over the period 1928 to 1947. In 1960 he had 6·5 times the chance—a very slight increase. All the evidence indicates that after the Robbins expansion the social composition of the student body in higher education stayed much as before. However, the increased numbers of students, and particularly those from working-class backgrounds, shows that there has been a small but tangible increase in educational opportunity. More important than the social composition of those at university has been the expansion of opportunity in further education and the increase in voluntary staying on at school beyond the statutory school-leaving age. In 1961 22·8 per cent of 15–17 year olds were in some form of further education establishment. In 1969 the comparable figure was 23·9 per cent. At the same time (1969) 42 per cent of the age group stayed on at school; therefore 41 per cent of those who had left school were utilising further education provision. In 1969 47 per cent of school-leavers were 16 or over; the comparable figure ten years earlier was 23 per cent. The 16–18 age-group shows the change in educational opportunity for working-class young people most clearly. It is in this area, however, particularly non-advanced further education, that the effects of government cuts in public expenditure have been most sharply felt. Despite these there has been a small improvement.

What of the future? There is no immediate prospect of any reform in the highly discriminatory access patterns of the colleges and universities. The causes of this discrimination are so deeply rooted in the social and economic fabric of the country that very radical or revolutionary measures will be needed to make an effective impact. This same fabric must be transformed so that the status and position of the working class in society is raised. Vastly increased levels of expenditure and altered admission requirements are likewise necessary. So although it can be argued that a little progress has been made, the basic problems remain. The situation will not improve with the developments that may well take place in the next decade—sharp cuts in expenditure and the declining value of student grants.

## Women and post-school education

Mention was made in the previous section of the differential inequality of access for women into higher education. This is repeated in all parts of post-school education. As the traditional housewife role of women becomes increasingly obsolete, as the number of qualified female school-leavers increases and as proportionately the economic role of women grows, this inequality will become more and more intolerable.

Approximately 40 per cent of students in full-time higher education are women, yet their number is strongly concentrated in the arts and social science subjects. Science and technology subjects are particularly weak in female representation. In 1970 there were 8,142 male students in CNAA engineering/technology degree courses and only 103 women; 4,007 students in science degree courses and 756 women. Career and employment opportunities for women students are more limited than for men. For day-release and industrial training the situation is much worse; 38·8 per cent of boys in employment between the ages of 16 and 18 benefited from day-release, but only one-quarter as many young women, 10·1 per cent, were on day-release. And this figure obscures the very low specific percentages in certain industries—insurance, banking, textiles, clothing and footwear were all well under 5 per cent in 1970. Accordingly, young women have less opportunity for career advancement and the acquisition of skills. For the majority of young women the choice is between housework and menial employment without prospects.

It is not the purpose of this book to examine in detail the reasons for this inequality. Certainly society in general, parents and the schools socialise and educate girls not to expect the same career and employment opportunities as men. The origins and roots of the discrimination are very deep, and like the class discrimination referred to before, the measures and actions necessary to deal with it fully will have to be correspondingly radical. What is positive in the present situation is that the student movement and the Labour movement are beginning to treat the question with the seriousness it merits.

Not so the DES or the Government: the recently produced *Training for the Future* made no reference to the industrial training problems facing women. The DES document *EPP2* in 1970 assumed that the proportion of qualified women succeeding in obtaining higher education places would fall by 1981. The 1972 White Paper proposed a 50 per cent cut in teacher training places. Teacher education has always been one of the major avenues for women securing higher education. Such a cut can only make access for women to higher education much more selective than it is already.

## The binary system

This term has a wide currency and refers to the divided nature of the system of higher and further education. The primary division is between the universities on the one hand, and all other institutions of post-school education, on the other. Reflecting wider social and economic class divisions and producing some very harmful educational effects, it has long been opposed by students and condemned by nearly all teachers' organisations, the House of Commons Public Expenditure Committee and many others.

The origins of the binary system are almost as old as the universities. Universities have always sought to be élite academic institutions. Accordingly, other institutions have had to be set up to meet the educational needs that the universities have been unable to cater for. Such needs are primarily in certain vocational areas and for lower level and part-time work. Gradually this state of affairs became more systematic as the state took an increasingly important involvement in the planning and financing of education. In the 1944 Education Act there is no mention made of the universities at all, whereas further education is defined as all education taking place beyond the statutory school-leaving age. It charged LEA's with certain responsibilities for further and adult education. The 1956 White Paper set up Colleges of Advanced Technology with direct access to central government funds. This as much as anything else laid the basis for one of the essential principles of binary policies—the rapid development of higher education outside the universities. In more conventional terms, however, the origin of an explicit and articulated policy resides with Mr. Crosland, who in April 1965 committed the Labour Government to the development of a dual system of higher education, the universities and the public sector being "separate but equal". At the time this was vigorously opposed by members of the Robbins Committee, a range of liberal university opinion and the NUS. Since then higher and further education has developed along the lines charted by Mr. Crosland. This policy was endorsed by the Conservative Government in its 1972 White

Paper. And irrespective of the policies developed by the Labour Party in opposition it now seems that the new Labour Government is carrying on where the old one left off.

The binary system divides post-school education into private and public sectors (the word "private" is in part a misnomer because the universities are not privately financed institutions). The private sector comprises the universities, forty-four institutions having more than one-half of the students on degree courses within them. They are separately financed from national resources through the University Grants Committee. They are chartered institutions; this conferring on them the right to award degrees and a wide area of academic self-government not possessed by other institutions. They do not pursue, with a few very notable exceptions such as Birkbeck College and the special case of the Open University, part-time or sub-degree level work. The bulk of research work sponsored by public agencies outside government departments themselves takes place in the universities. Relative to the polytechnics and colleges they are high status institutions, first in the pecking order and usually first choice for suitably qualified school-leavers. They have generally better facilities and more money at their disposal, while their academic staff are better paid and have better career opportunities.

Students in the public sector ("public" meaning those colleges and polytechnics that are maintained and controlled by LEA's) are made to feel that a class distinction exists between themselves and students in the universities. The system is irrational and wasteful, as is shown by the following quotation from the NUS document "Higher Education in the 1970's":

> "in one area of London it has been estimated that a student travelling by public transport from one part of his polytechnic to another part will pass outside three separate university institutions; whether he will be allowed inside to attend a lecture or to use the refectory, the library or the common room, is a problem which, judging by student experience elsewhere, will involve years of argument and negotiation leading to an unsuccessful conclusion."

True, one can talk of a class distinction only in a notional sense. But the divisions between different sectors and institutions reflect and are appropriate to a class-divided society, itself based on the division and conflict between those who own and control substantial wealth and those who do not.

Library provision in universities is better than in the polytechnics and colleges. Bookstock is considerably larger. In 1967 the Libraries Association found that there were 12·5 books and bound periodicals extant per student in polytechnics and 150 per student in universities. The situation has not markedly improved since then. Average student union fees for university unions are considerably more than for polytechnics and colleges of education. (Average university union fees are now some £16 per annum, polytechnics £10–12 and £4·75 for colleges of education.) University unions usually have much more accommodation at their disposal than their public sector equivalents. Though it is difficult to compare exactly the staff/student ratios in different sectors, it is clear that they are better in the universities.

The status and salary/career attraction of the universities ensures that they recruit from the public sector. Between 1962 and 1968 40 per cent of the expansion of student numbers in universities were accommodated in halls of residence built for the purpose. In colleges of education the proportion was only 12 per cent, in the polytechnics 10 per cent.

Polytechnics have a generally higher failure and dropout rate than the universities, and students spend more hours being taught and less in private study than their university counterparts. Such is the retinue of inequality and the vacuity of Mr. Crosland's "separate but equal".

The binary system does not, however, present a straight dividing line. Divisions exist within particular sectors and between age-groups and institutions catering for different levels of course. Art and Design education has its own hierarchy with the "big three" at the top—the Royal College of Art, the Slade School of Fine Art and the Royal Academy Schools. Further education is divided between polytechnics largely catering for advanced, over 18, full-time and degree work, and the colleges of further education and area colleges catering for lower level, 16 to 19, day-release, part-time and evening work. The polytechnics have sharply reduced their commitment to lower level work in recent years. Oxford and Cambridge have their special niche in the university sector. Perhaps the most important and divisive distinction, apart from the public-private one, is that between advanced and non-advanced work. Staff teaching advanced-course students are better paid, have lighter teaching loads and have more opportunities for research. Students studying on advanced courses (with a few absurd exceptions) receive mandatory awards, grants that are automatic on acceptance to a course and guaranteed in level (assuming any parental contribution is paid). By comparison, students on non-advanced courses receive lower level grants at the discretion of LEA's and can be completely without support.

What is the justification of the binary system? It is rarely argued for as a policy, and arguments put up are often contradictory. In 1965 Mr. Crosland gave three reasons: that it was desirable to have an element of higher education under "social", i.e. LEA control; that a unitary system would be bad for the morale of institutions outside the universities; and that the public sector was more responsive than the universities to social and industrial pressures and to student demand. There can be no doubt that the DES mandarinate, and particularly Mr. Toby Weaver, had a profound and guiding influence on the development of the binary policy. Higher and further education has never been the most politically important part of the education system to Ministers, and so civil servants have a proportionately greater say. Crosland argues in *The Politics of Education* (Penguin 1971), p. 193, that the civil servants misled him—"I had only a superficial knowledge of the subject. . . ." Is this Crosland trying to blame the civil servants for his own shortcomings—or were Weaver & Co. taking advantage? Probably there is truth in both.

LEA control is increasingly inappropriate for large institutions of higher education. The LEA's exert a restrictive influence. The argument about morale is false because the existing system is buttressed by status distinctions which are harmful to the morale of the public sector. As for the universities not being responsive to social and industrial pressures, there is a marked desire for commercial sponsorship of research projects in the university sector. Some of the most vocational subjects, e.g. medicine and theology, can only be studied in universities. Binary exponents, like George Brosan, Director of North-East London Polytechnic, support it on the grounds that there is an inherent difference between practical-type and theoretical-type subjects. Eric Robinson said in 1966: "I support this policy because by maintaining and developing all levels of work in the public sector, it lays the basis of a comprehensive system of the type I envisage. A suitably developed public system could absorb the universities at a later stage." He was referring to the polytechnics which very soon began shedding the lower level work he was anxious to preserve. He further advocated the Government's polytechnics policy on the grounds that the main strategic objective of a radical higher educational policy was the "smashing" of the universities. Government action on the one hand and the dynamism of the polytechnics on the other would comprise a pincer movement. Bigger polytechnics will not, however, make the removal of the binary system easier. They will simply make its continued existence more absurd.

There seem to be in fact four reasons for the continuation of the binary system:

1. The inertia of the *status quo*—"like Topsy it just grow'd" as a result of a multiplicity of pressures. In particular the LEA's are anxious to retain their stake in higher education. The inertia of the Department of Education and Science contributes to the maintenance of the structure.

2. The binary system with its conflicting and competing interests serves the Government and the DES well. The divide and rule tactic is extremely useful, especially when there is a fight for limited funds.

3. The Government probably thinks that polytechnics are cheaper institutions to expand than universities in terms of unit student and staff costs. There may be some validity in this when, for example, the amounts of library and student residence provision are compared. However, in polytechnics there is a higher wastage rate while in the universities the greater amount of research work undertaken will distort any simple equation. At a wider level, the very duplication of facilities that the binary system creates means that the whole exercise is very expensive indeed.

4. The students leaving polytechnics and public sector institutions are thought by some to be better equipped to live in the "real" world,

more amenable to employers, in possession of more marketable qualifications, etc. There is certainly some truth in this—probably as much because the polytechnics are relatively new and not so encrusted with traditional patterns of courses as are universities. However, the difference between a technological university, e.g., Brunel, and a polytechnic in this regard evades all but the most devout supporters of the binary system.

None of these can provide any valid educational basis for the binary system. Yet it remains the basic plank of higher education policy, for it has been decided to build up the polytechnics and effectively preclude colleges of education amalgamating with the universities. This is a divisive policy, producing gross institutional and educational inequalities and very wasteful of public money.

### Non-advanced further education

Non-advanced further education is by far the largest sector of post-school education. There are over three million full and part-time students and a total of more than 700 further education and technical colleges involved. It compares very sharply with higher education, the part of post-school education which is post-18 and requires "A" levels or an equivalent entry "ticket". Entry to non-advanced further education is less restrictive in terms of educational attainment, the major limitation being finance and facilities. The variety of courses provided are far greater than in any other part of post-school education—part-time and full-time, day-release and evening-only, "A" levels and "O" levels, ONC and HNC, hairdressing and bricklaying, law and accountancy, the recreational, the academic and the strictly vocational—all with wide variations according to local requirements. Socially and educationally this sector has acted as an alternative educational opportunity for some of those who failed in the school system, and an additional and very valuable access route to higher education. Equally important, the further education and technical colleges provide instruction and a related education for young workers in industry, responding closely to the needs of employers for a trained labour force. This is largely catered for through day-release, sandwich and block-release courses. The third and increasingly important function is the provision of adult and recreational studies.

The diversity of further education is so great that, viewed from a national perspective, it seems more like incoherence. The main reason for this is the almost total lack of Government policy in the area, still less priority. Inadequate funds, and the willingness of LEA's and the DES to prune the educational budget in this area at times of economic stress, have contributed to its unsystematic development. Yet ironically this chronic neglect has given the further education colleges a measure of freedom to innovate educationally which other areas of post-school education, tightly linked to performance in school-leaving examinations, do not possess. The absence of priority is shown by the fact that the Robbins Report ignored non-advanced further education, while the 1966 Polytechnic White Paper concentrated entirely on advanced work and the Education Expenditure White Paper of the Tory Government accorded only a fleeting mention. This White Paper charted out a plan of capital development for the polytechnics at the expense of further education colleges. Further Education as a whole (including advanced and non-advanced elements) has a single capital development programme. The polytechnic sector consumed 36 per cent of this in 1972–3 and is planned to absorb 59 per cent in 1973–4. There are thirty polytechnics and over 650 further education institutions which this year will between them consume a minority of the further education budget. This is but one aspect of the Government's thoroughly divisive policy of playing off one sector of education against another. Another way of showing Government priority is to compare the total capital and recurrent expenditure on universities in 1971–2 (£417·3m) with that of further education (both parts)—£416·7m.

In the last decade the development of non-advanced further education has been small as compared with higher education. In a period of time when the number of students in full time higher education doubled, the number of students on day release declined, from 261,380 in 1962 to 243,945 in 1970. Although the number of young people in employment under 18 also declined, and the proportion of them on day-release increased, the number is totally inadequate when measured against the modest half-million figure recommended for 1970 by the Henniker-Heaton Committee in 1964. As with higher education, the situation for young women is appreciably worse than it is for young men. In 1970 the proportion of young male workers released for one day a week was 38·2 per cent, for women this figure was only 9·6 per cent.

How does non-advanced further education fare for the student? There are as many impressions, problems and attitudes as there are courses. Student union provision in the majority of further education colleges is quite inadequate. College authorities seem to regard student unions as unnecessary or subversive. LEA's are unwilling to pay sufficient money to allow unions to function properly. This situation is exacerbated by the very high turnover of students—so many being part-time or on short courses—and the relative youth and inexperience of the students. Building a strong and viable union in these circumstances is not easy. Most authorities either do not care or seek to run the union themselves through senior or staff treasurers. Student grants are atrocious and by their paucity of number and level prevent many from starting and others from completing their studies. Awards are in the main given at the discretion of LEA's and few exercise this with any comparability to those available for degree level courses. Student representation in academic government is insufficient, despite a number of important recent developments following the DES Circular 7/70. Although some of the teaching is very progressive, authoritarian attitudes and a concern for instruction rather than education often prevail and match the inadequate student representation. In other circumstances almost no co-ordination of education can be the rule (each teacher "doing his own thing"), a state of affairs where a diverse teaching force can create confusion and uncertainty for students. Despite their potential for educational flexibility, the further-education colleges and technical colleges meet the needs of employers more than they meet the needs of young workers—a clear purpose can be seen to the authoritarianism mentioned above.

## Polytechnics

Many institutions which are now polytechnics had their origins as colleges of the sort mentioned in the previous section. In 1966, given an overall binary policy and an expanding demand for higher education, it was desirable to concentrate existing advanced work in further education into a limited number of institutions. The Government argued (but their argument has never been adequately proven) that this was a more efficient way of organising scarce resources as compared with letting advanced work develop in a much larger number of institutions of further education. Accordingly some thirty polytechnics were designated. The word "promotion" has been used because throughout the modern history of higher education there has been a marked tendency for technical colleges to be "elevated". A number of the large civic universities began life as mechanics' institutes in the nineteenth century. The 1956 Government White Paper on Technical Education classified technical colleges into four sorts—local, area, regional and national according to their catchment area of student intake. At the same time a number of leading technical colleges were taken out of the further education sector and made into Colleges of Advanced Technology with direct access to Government funds. These CAT's then became Technological Universities as a result of the Robbins Report. The results of this Football League approach to higher education are that the non-advanced and part-time work outside the reorganisation or change of status remains relatively impoverished of funds and facilities, unbalanced in its teaching force and bereft of overall policy, guidance or status. The advanced students and their teachers, too, do not always benefit from being removed from areas of work with which they were closely associated.

One of the main attractions in the early period of development of polytechnics (1967–70) was that they seemed to have the potential of becoming comprehensive institutions, in the sense that they catered for a wide variety and level of courses, full and part-time—as opposed to the universities which dealt with degree-level and postgraduate work only. Indeed, Labour ministers attempting to find arguments for the policy they had adopted delighted in making this point. It seemed to "out-left the left" which was criticising the policy and arguing for comprehensive reorganisation at the post-16 and post-18 levels. However, it did not take long for this argument to wear thin and the old pattern of the promotion race to reassert itself. The polytechnics began shedding their lower level courses and becoming almost entirely concerned with advanced level work. There are a number of reasons for this sad development. The LEA's which maintain the polytechnics, the Directors and some of the academic staff desire status above all else—ultimately some want university designation. The system of financing allows advanced work to command more money than non-advanced work—higher salaries, better career prospects and wider research opportunities for staff. The fact that advanced work is centrally financed through a pool contributed to by every LEA in the country gives the polytechnics relatively more freedom from the purse-strings of the maintaining LEA's than they would otherwise have (LEA's like this too because it means that they individually pay less for courses in their own polytechnic). And finally the DES was in favour of it, because it was in line with their "promotion" policy.

At the time of the 1966 White Paper the NUS welcomed the formation of polytechnics and, in passing, expressed some concern that matters of student discipline, representation and union autonomy should be properly catered for (in a way they had not been when the new universities were set up a few years earlier). This was unfortunate, for the overall anti-binary stance of the Union implied a more hostile position. However, the leadership at the time probably calculated that nothing would stop the Government setting up its polytechnics, and that as politics is "the art of the possible", the best thing to do was to compliment the Government and hope that some sops would come their way. The Association of Teachers in Technical Institutions, as the other main body concerned, likewise accepted the polytechnics policy but placed a very severe qualification on it, stating that it was in favour of other technical and further education colleges being able to develop advanced work. It challenged the central nostrum of the White Paper that it was somehow more efficient (vague arguments about "economics of scale") to concentrate advanced work at a limited number of centres. After all, they argued, some universities had tiny departments and nobody worried about their "efficiency", likewise many school sixth forms were very small.

Since their designation the polytechnics have expanded more rapidly than any other sector of higher education. They appeared to receive favoured nation treatment, with lavish ministerial pronouncements and some money. Yet their subjection to "productivity-type" investigations—particularly the three reports of the Pilkington Committee (a sub-committee investigating the use of technical college facilities)—in association with an overall gross cash shortage, has meant overcrowding and inadequate facilities for many. The Ministry intends them to expand very rapidly in future and in all probability their present problems will be exacerbated.

Since 1966 the polytechnics have been "sold" extensively by commercial advertising and ministerial speeches. The main public relations argument has been that they are more up-to-date and provide more relevant courses and qualifications for students than the universities, their technology and social science courses being supposedly more sought after by "industry". This has had an attraction for some students, though in the main there is still a marked preference for universities amongst school-leavers. Lex Donaldson (*Higher Education Review*, Spring 1973), interpreting a survey of students undertaken at the Enfield precinct of Middlesex Polytechnic, concluded that a large number of respondents regarded the education received at a polytechnic as being more socially relevant than a university's. However, in every other respect—openness of curricula, career opportunities, etc.—the students saw no difference between the two sectors. This conclusion would need to be compared with the attitudes of students at universities before it can be regarded as definitive. The publicity the polytechnics have received and the greater difficulty that now exists in getting to university in a number of subjects are important factors determining the attitudes of students.

Though facilities in polytechnics are not as good as those in the universities, in a number of ways they have played a very important role for the student body as a whole. As far as student discipline, union autonomy and representation are concerned the polytechnic students secured a better deal than students at the new universities (both those that were completely new and those that were previously CAT's). Important though by no means revolutionary changes in these three areas were written into the Instruments and Articles of Government of the polytechnics as a result of pressures from students in 1966–8. These then became a model for students in colleges of education and technical colleges. In the last three or four years development of polytechnic unions has been particularly rapid, the numbers of sabbatical officers and the level of student union fees in some cases having doubled or trebled. This is fortunate because a secure organisational basis will be essential for students in the future development of the polytechnics.

## College of Education

"The saddest part of all this is that these three years could have been very profitable had we been sufficiently stimulated to study for ourselves and to forget the monotonous lectures—often regurgitations of books we could have read for ourselves, but were never required to" (Linda Tinckham, *Student Power*, Penguin 1969).

The Colleges of Education began in the nineteenth century as institutions set up by the churches in order to train teachers for the elementary schools they ran. This isolated and introverted aspect of the colleges remains with them to this day. It was only in 1902 that the Local Authorities began to play any role in teacher training. The courses initially offered by the colleges were one or two years in duration. Only in 1960 was a three-year course introduced. The colleges have been notoriously small-sized institutions compared with other colleges and universities. In 1939 there were 83 training colleges, 64 of which had less than 150 students, and 28 less than 100. Even now (outside Scotland) there are only 22 colleges with over 1,000 students.

These weaknesses make the history of the colleges one of subservience to voluntary bodies, LEA's, the universities and the DES. The colleges more than any other sector of higher education have never been deemed to be sufficiently competent to award their own qualifications. This and the colleges' own timidity have led them to accept a big brother relationship with the universities. Since 1944 the colleges have existed under the academic umbrella of university institutes of education—nominally federations, but with the universities quite clearly holding the ring. The Robbins Report recommended that the colleges of education should have a proportion of their students on degree courses, the B.Ed. Since that time the number of students leaving college with the B.Ed. has gradually increased and this has led to a greater self-respect and an element of freedom in the colleges. However, more than anything else the B.Ed. has shown up the inconsistencies and inadequacies of university tutelage. Some universities award the B.Ed. with honours, others do not. Some require those admitted to the B.Ed. to have obtained requisite "A" level passes. One university has refused to award a B.Ed. under any circumstances. Such variations are pre-posterous monuments to university "academic freedom", for teaching is a nationally determined profession and teachers and students should have the same opportunities in all parts of the country.

The Colleges of Education are more rigidly controlled than any other sector of higher education. They exist in a veritable vice. The universities are responsible for academic validation, the LEA's or voluntary bodies for the overall running and development of the colleges, while the DES rigorously decides the number of students who will be admitted and the broad categories of student (those to teach in primary schools, secondary schools, etc). In 1965 the Secretary of State told the colleges that they would have to increase their "output" by 20 per cent with no increase in capital funds available, which they did scarcely with a whimper—to the detriment of their students. No other sector could have been so instructed.

In the late 1960's changing student requirements and altered professional and educational needs led to a crisis in the colleges. Their small size (and questionable viability as higher educational institutions), structural position and history of subservience and sponsorship, paternalistic approach to students and largely monotechnic and monosexual character, all came under attack. It was absurd for there to be separate colleges for men and women and for student teachers to be isolated from other sections of the student body—students are still largely unable to transfer on to other courses or take up anything but the narrowest educational options. (In only five colleges is it possible to take degrees not of the B.Ed. variety; only one college trains teachers/nurses on a five-year course; only one college runs a joint year of a course with a university, a human biology course at Surrey University.) They are deprived of social and educational intercourse with their fellow students. Such colleges were seen as totally unsatisfactory places for the education of teachers. Their only justification could be that the DES needed administrative control over teacher supply and an apprentice teaching force with narrow employment options, so that salaries could be artificially depressed.

A wide ranging and profoundly critical debate about teacher education took place. The result of this was an official enquiry conducted by a committee chaired by Lord James. In retrospect one can see the recent history of teacher education as an astute move by the Conservative Party in opposition and in government. Nothing was to be lost by meeting the demand of the critics for an enquiry—they probably gained a few votes in the 1970 election. The report itself was so bad that even the Government had to reject its central recommendations. This gave them the initiative. Mrs. Thatcher was much more concerned with nursery education than anything else (again in part for easy electoral reasons) and thought that with present student numbers in training there would be a gross surplus of teachers in 1981, given projections of a further decline in the birth rate. Accordingly, her answer to the problems of teacher education was to reduce student numbers from

114,000 to 65,000 in 1981. Some colleges will close or become in service training centres for teachers. A few will join polytechnics. Some of the larger colleges with CNAA validated degrees and the Dip.HE., may be able to become polytechnic type colleges. For the majority the educational and professional problems will remain a financial climate not conducive to innovation. This has been the tragic record of the last few years. They were expanded at governmental whim in the 1960's, then chopped back in the 1970's. The movement for reform was bought off with an enquiry and now the colleges and lecturers seem more concerned with saving their own skins.

From a student point of view the colleges are generally unsatisfactory institutions. They have a history of authoritarianism which has only recently begun to change. In the area of hall of residence regulations college students still have less freedom over visiting hours than their colleagues in polytechnics and universities. Student representation is generally at a low level and union financing is poor. There have been some positive moves. All but twenty of the colleges are now mixed (though this is only nominal in many), and some colleges have attempted to secure CNAA recognition for their B.Ed. degrees and move away from the restrictive university umbrella. Yet in some colleges there is a rather disconcerting and vacuous liberalism, where principals and senior staff are trying hard to propagate educational reform and generate the environment of an institution of higher education. But when in the last analysis the DES holds all the cards it is an almost impossible task. Yet in common with other students, those in the colleges have become more active and militant in the last few years.

The future of the colleges is bleak. With the effects of the cuts on the already draconian White Paper and the fact that a future Government will have to reverse the disastrous teacher supply target of 65,000 students in the colleges by 1981 (unless there are to be even more serious staffing problems in the schools than there now are), a debilitating and protracted crisis in the colleges seems likely. This cannot help the students or teachers grappling with the problem of producing better educated and trained teachers. The basic reason for this situation is that the Government has always wanted to have an administratively separate sector of higher education whose numbers it can rigidly manipulate as a central element of the binary policy. Giving student teachers parity with other students would make it less likely that a number would enter the teaching profession at the present salary levels. Similarly, the colleges cannot be allowed to diversify their courses significantly and gain the independence this entails. If the LEA's as employers of teachers and the DES had to compete more actively with other employers for teachers, much more money would have to be spent on teachers, salaries and their conditions of work. The DES has always preferred the educationally self-defeating "Passchendaele policy" of teacher supply. It is cheaper to educate many teachers and provide them with a relatively cheaper form of higher education (thereby soaking up educational demand) and then lose them. An increasingly young profession costs much less than an older and more experienced one and teacher union organisation is also weakened with a rapid turnover of membership (married women returners with family commitments are difficult to organise).

The uncertain future of the colleges means that they will not be able to discharge their major responsibilities: producing better educated and trained teachers, assisting teachers in service and providing a focal point for the generation of new ideas. Of one thing we can be certain. Their position in the system of higher education will be crucial. Now they are vital to the preservation of the binary system. They provide the numerical, strategic and institutional balance between the universities and the polytechnics. Teacher education could be the crucial catalytic agent of educational reform in a comprehensive reorganisation of post-school education.

## The art colleges

This sector of higher and further education has been an area where substantial curricular and educational experimentation has been possible. At the same time, paradoxically, it has been subject to close scrutiny and control by the Department of Education and Science. Until 1962, when the Diploma of Art and Design was instituted, the Department, in addition to having overall financial and administrative control over the colleges, actually marked the examination scripts of the major art and design qualification—the National Diploma in Design.

Art and design education has remained in splendid institutional isolation. And this produces the desired political weakness of the sector *vis-à-vis* the Department. The bohemian isolation of art education represents an attitude sedulously fostered in British capitalist society—that art and design activities are peripheral and incidental to the main business of life and the economy. The process of education for the mass of people is primarily concerned with numeracy and literacy and only marginally with the development of aesthetic dimensions to human experience. Even today many regard art as a minority and rather eccentric pursuit or a perennial and interesting recreation financed by bourgeois patronage. Design, on the other hand, is regarded as an élite activity at the service of manufacturers as anxious to stimulate and titillate the market as to produce good and attractive products. In the absence of Ministerial interest, the civil servants responsible for art and design education have little concern apart from cost saving and the preservation of the status quo.

All this is borne out in the developments of the last ten years. Warren-Piper (*Readings in Art and Design Education, II*) has shown that in the period 1959–69 the number of students in full-time art establishments increased by 46·3 per cent, whereas in full-time grant-aided establishments in general the increase was 122·4 per cent. The proportion of full-time students in art and design education compared with full-time students as a whole has sharply declined in the last decade. Entry to Diploma in Art and Design courses has become much more competitive in the same period. Paralleling this relative run-down of opportunities in art and design education has been the closure or absorption of many colleges. Between 1960 and 1967 twenty-seven, or 15 per cent of all art establishments closed. The main effect of this has been felt by non-advanced recreational and part-time work. Diploma studies have been largely protected within the polytechnic framework. It can be argued that many of the very small foundation colleges were isolated, inefficient, out of touch, conservative and not at all the *avant garde* centres that some of their supporters have maintained. But all the same, their systematic closure as a matter of unstated policy is perturbing.

In September 1970 the Report of the Joint Working Party was published. It had been charged to look into the whole fabric of art and design education and propose reforms. Set up in part as a result of the troubles of 1968, many hoped that it would make some radical recommendations. These hopes were dashed, for the report could almost have been written by the DES rather than the Working Party. It ignored the major questions raised in 1968 and made recommendations directly counter to what students and progressive staff had demanded. Its main proposals were: to split the Dip.AD. into "A" and "B" parts—the former fine art based and the latter oriented towards industrial design; to rationalise vocational sub-diploma level courses by the institution of a new type of course leading to the Design Technician Certificate; to institute sandwich courses on a much wider scale in the art colleges for the purported needs of industry and commerce; to suggest that foundation studies could be by-passed for a number of Diploma students and that entry could be direct from school sixth forms; and to maintain existing GCE entry requirements for diploma studies. The report exhibited a compartmentalised and very narrow approach in thinking that the Dip.AD. could be split along an academic/vocational line. It made no attempt to justify the maintenance of GCE entrance requirements. Still less did it demand a programme of expansion to restore comparability with other sectors.

The furore this report created led the Government to reject some of its major proposals. DES circular 7/71 made some concessions to the opinions raised. In particular "A" and "B" Diplomas were rejected and the long-established moratorium (since 1957) on the development of new diploma courses was lifted. However, the politics of the situation were similar to the débâcle of the James Report, and the DES retained the tactical advantage. The scenario might almost be described as follows: set up the type of enquiry that all the radicals are obliged to spend a lot of time attacking, concede that they are right and reject the report, then you have the initiative and can do relatively unimpeded what you wanted to do all along. The issues raised in 1968 and so inadequately dealt with by the Joint Working Party Report were shelved, and art education remained largely unreformed.

Particularly important for art education is the question of GCE entrance requirements. The folly of dependence on GCE results for admission is demonstrated more clearly than in any other sector of higher education. The practice is rarely defended. There are three reasons for it: to give art and design education degree "status', to bring it in line with the grants regulations, and to limit access. Not one relates to the content of art and design education. No one has ever adequately demonstrated any educational correlation between performance in "A" and "O" levels and competence as an artist or designer, or as an art or design student. Despite the oft-quoted "exception clause" that lets in the "illiterate Leonardo" with no GCE's, many are denied access when they could benefit from an art and design education. The rigid entry requirements are necessary because of the totally inadequate expansion of the last decade.

What of the future? The Government has seen to it that diploma studies will largely take place within the polytechnics for reasons of "rationalisation", "efficient use of plant" and "responding to the needs of industry". One fine artist, Patrick Heron, has even referred to the "murder of art education" at the hands of the polytechnics. It is essential that art and design education at diploma level be allowed to develop outside the polytechnics. For work below diploma level a working party is at present looking into the relevance of the "design technician concept" and proposed practice. Overall there is no Government policy—except containment and continue as before. This affects the lower level and part time work worst of all.

Art students, as was demonstrated in 1968, are among the most volatile of the student body. They are also the least well provided for in terms of union finance and facilities. This in part relates to the intensely individualistic approach of many art students to their work. At the same time there is a strength of commitment to education and innovation which is very valuable to the student body as a whole.

As with teacher education, art education could make a unique, dynamic and creative contribution to any comprehensive reform of post-school education. Its isolation, degradation and internal élitism would then be abolished. Art and design activities could become an element of many higher education courses. The art students, too, could benefit from this arrangement. For contact and co-operation with wider sections of the student body and with other disciplines might be very much more productive than merely having an ersatz general studies slot in the timetable.

### The universities

To many the universities *are* higher education and students by definition are university students. This view reflects the leading position that these institutions occupy in post-school education and in education generally. They are the oldest, most autonomous, best financed, largest (as institutions and as a sector) and most powerful institutions of higher education. They have a pervasive influence on the rest of the education system. The Robbins Report, as stated earlier, was a university biased report in as far as it sought to preserve and enhance their status. Though they have been challenged from a number of quarters in the last decade, their position has been maintained and in some ways strengthened. Despite Government concentration on the polytechnics, the binary policy necessitates the maintenance of the universities' position as "top dog". At a personal level there can be few senior civil servants or Government ministers responsible for education who would seriously contemplate not sending their children to university, and most would insist on Oxbridge.

University student numbers expanded from 98,400 in 1962 to 236,000 in 1971. As important in this period was the establishment and rapid development of a number of new universities—Lancaster, Sussex, Essex, Warwick, Kent, Stirling and York, together with the technological universities from the CAT's—Surrey, Heriot-Watt, Strathclyde, UWIST, City, Brunel, Bradford, Salford and Aston. Sussex and Keele had been established earlier. All of them were as a matter of policy established on greenfield sites as opposed to urban ones. No doubt it was cheaper to obtain land and plan for the future in such locations, but I strongly believe that the decision of the Conservative Government in 1963 may well prove to have been one of the worst educational decisions of the century. The idea behind their siting was an out-of-date "Oxbridge" one, that higher learning, professional training (in so far as it is undertaken by the universities) and research are best conducted in a semi-monastic context. This is further borne out by the fact that three of the new universities adopted an Oxbridge-type collegiate structure. They have contributed somewhat to the innovation of curricula and course structures by their mixed degree courses, newer types of teaching methods, etc. It would be calamitous if they had not done this, given the opportunities their formation created. However, in the public mind the new universities are most noted for student unrest. With the possible exception of York all have experienced profound and bitter conflicts and a type of student unrest which has been less organised, more bizarre and violent than the generality. What are the reasons for this?

1. The isolation of the campuses has made the student bodies more introverted and more "unbalanced" in their attitude towards the

community. Some writers have referred to a neurosis caused by "collective solitary confinement".

2. The authorities' reactions to tensions and challenge have been a potent cause of student unrest in all the institutions of higher education in the last six years, but have been more marked at the new universities. In a sense their very novelty may have encouraged it. The effects of expansion have been relatively greater than elsewhere.

3. The authorities from their inception sought to prevent strong unions developing. The idea, particularly evident at Essex, was to create an integrated and paternalistic community which would render unions unnecessary. At Lancaster, Kent and York this was to be done by a collegiate framework with Junior Common Rooms, college communities, etc. The result has been that students have had to resort to direct action because their representative organisation was not strong enough to take up their grievances.

4. Partly because of a large amount of media attention, the new universities have been "trendy" institutions. Student unrest can be "trendy" too.

5. Vice-Chancellors of these universities have invariably started out with an overall view of what their university was to be like. In this they have had more scope than those of older universities. They have tended to get annoyed when students or staff have challenged their scheme—and despite often liberal intentions, have reacted in an authoritarian manner.

It is my view that unless something radical is done to make the relationship between these universities and the community more balanced they are in danger of becoming "educational ghettoes" in the twenty-first century.

The influence of the universities over the institutions of higher education is one of the main forces maintaining the binary system. They represent a status to which the rest aspire. Mechanisms are various—the Institutes of Education for the colleges of education, representation on governing bodies of many public sector colleges, an overall responsibility through the examination boards for GCE examinations, the attraction for school-leavers wanting a higher education, representation on the Council for National Academic Awards and so on. Though they have successfully maintained their position the Government has not always supported them fully. In particular it has prevented schemes of closer co-operation or amalgamation between universities and public sector institutions. This has led to some highly irrational decisions, for example: in the mid-sixties not to allow any relationship to develop between Warwick University and the well established regional college—Lanchester College of Technology, barely five miles away in Coventry. More recently, a plan of reorganisation for four institutions of higher and further education at Loughborough, sharing the same site, has been turned down by the Government. Though this plan had serious weaknesses, in particular because it ignored lower level work, the DES would take no initiative in the matter.

Despite the fact that Vice-Chancellors complain that the university idea is being assailed by cost-conscious civil servants, governments wanting to use the universities for their own political purposes, student activists and miscellaneous egalitarians, their future place in the sun is guaranteed. The 1971 White Paper plans that there will be 375,000 students at universities in 1981 compared with 335,000 in advanced further education and the colleges of education. The universities will still have a majority of those in full-time higher education. At the time of its publication most educational organisations commented on the inadequacy of the Government student numbers target for 1981 and the fact that it had been decided to do nothing whatsoever about ending the binary system. The Vice-Chancellors said that the situation was as reasonable as might be expected in the circumstances. This is partly because they are not a radical group of men and because it would not be "right" to attack the Government on an issue like this. But as it will be more difficult than now for the average well-qualified school-leaver to secure access to university, the universities can and will be more selective about whom they decide to admit. Many in universities welcome this prospect.

### The influence of business and industry

No consideration of the structure of higher and further education is complete without an examination of the role and influence of business and industry. This is a very sensitive area and a few academics will even assert that there is no influence at all. On the other hand, some students on the left have asserted that the universities are little more than training grounds for particular skills required by the capitalists—an adjunct to the productive process. Both views are extreme. But it is clear that the needs and wishes of employers often have a pre-eminent role in the formulation of policies for higher and further education. As far as universities and their students are concerned two important objectionable examples of the involvement of big business have occurred in recent years—Warwick and Stirling. During an occupation at Warwick in February 1970 an investigation of the university's files revealed that Mr. Gilbert Hunt, the Chairman of the University Council, who was also the Chairman of Rootes (now Chrysler), had corresponded with the Vice-Chancellor of the University, J. Butterworth, about one, Dr. Montgomery. He was an American visiting member of staff at the university who had been in contact with Rootes shop-stewards (in speaking at a Coventry Labour Party meeting). Mr. Butterworth was informed that his activities in this direction were being watched. This was regarded by the students as the tip of an iceberg of business intervention in the university (business-financed chairs, emphasis on industry-orientated research, etc.). At Stirling the dispute arising out of the Queen's visit in October 1972 resulted in John Player's threatening that unless something was done about the students involved, a grant for a new sports centre would be withdrawn. These cases are both typical and atypical—typical in that big business works on a day-to-day basis with university authorities, but atypical in that big business does not normally have to resort to open intervention to secure what it wants from the universities. It is at times of crisis that the realities of political situations can become clearer. The interests of big business do not lie in the exposure of its substantial influence over higher education. It has to be maintained in subtle and perhaps confusing ways.

1. Employers are well represented on the boards of governors and councils of the colleges, polytechnics and universities; this gives them the possibility of a direct say in the running of each institution. Trade unions are also represented but not to the same extent. There is a closer

social contact between Principals and Vice-Chancellors and employers than there is with trade unions. College authorities are employers themselves.

2. Large firms in particular feel disposed for a variety of motives to finance chairs, build laboratories and sometimes halls of residence at universities. Such expenditure can yield direct rewards to the firm concerned and provide a valuable entrée for further benefit. At the same time it is good public relations to appear philanthropic.

3. Increasingly, universities and polytechnics tailor their research facilities to the variable needs of industry. Firms are induced to buy research because there is a shortage of public money to finance research. With every new economic crisis cuts in the budgets of the research councils are made and the universities and polytechnics are forced to look elsewhere. It corresponds to the Government's research policy—the customer/contractor principle as enunciated in the 1972 Rothschild Report. According to this, the customer, basically the state or industry, should determine what is researched. It is, of course, particularly clear in relation to Ministry of Defence and Pentagon contracts. MOD spent £1·7m on college-based research in 1973, the Pentagon 228,000 dollars. Most universities have themselves established consultancy arrangements to assist big business. There is a long history of universities themselves setting up companies to market the results of research, e.g., the Pye Instrument Company in Cambridge, University presses, computer companies, etc.

4. Industry as a major employer of graduates exerts a direct and indirect influence on the objectives and content of courses. This is shown most clearly in relation to postgraduate business studies courses. One of the implicit assumptions on which many courses are based is to prepare students for employment of a particular sort—why else have courses, some would say? Industry poses variable demands on higher education. Sometimes it is stated that graduates are not sufficiently specialised and competent in narrow disciplines, though Sir Paul Chambers, then Chairman of ICI, said in the 1964 Chuter Ede Lecture that industry wanted no more than well educated and experienced people—his company could train them in specific skills. On the other

hand, GKN in its evidence to the Parliamentary Expenditure Committee in 1972 asserted that students were not sufficiently conscious of the needs of industry. Clearly there is a variation from industry to industry, within particular industries, and according to the size of the concern. Some capitalists now think that a commission in the armed forces is a good preparation, presumably because of expertise in "man management" or controlling uppity workers. Army officers' values are thought to be less suspect than the graduate's.

5. The Confederation of British Industry and the Conservative Party are supported by private enterprise in order to pursue their objectives at a political level. The CBI through lobbying and backdoor methods exerts a degree of influence on the DES. This influence is not always as great as sometimes imagined. The Dip.HE., the Government's pet proposal for higher education in the 1972 White Paper, did not meet with the support of the CBI beforehand. The latter argued that for the employers there was already sufficient variety of output from the colleges and universities, further education and the sixth forms. However, the Government, with a mind no doubt to the overall maintenance of a capitalist society, public expenditure priorities and the provision of higher education—rather than merely manpower supply—went ahead with its scheme. Manpower planning studies are embarked upon from time to time by the DES with the needs of employers uppermost. Their success has been variable.

6. The setting up of new institutions with new types of courses is an important means of meeting the changing needs of industry. At the beginning of this century the civic universities were established to meet the new commercial and imperial requirements of the time (vide Joseph Chamberlain as the founder of Birmingham University). In 1956 the CAT's were set up and a decade later the polytechnics and technological universities. Since the CAT's were established the favourite mechanism of meeting industrial requirements has been the sandwich course. Both polytechnics and technological universities have much emphasised it. It is easier to respond to new requirements by setting up new colleges and universities. For this avoids confrontation with established academic interests.

7. The position of non-advanced further education must not be ignored. For skilled workers and technicians the technical colleges have an indispensable role in providing day-release, the most obviously vocational post-school education. The technical and further education colleges attempt to meet the needs of employment in a more direct way than any other sector. At the same time the skills acquired by students and employers are of central importance. As stated at the outset, the question is not straightforward. It is very important that students are able to be employed when they leave college or university. It is also vital that they are educated and not merely vocationally trained. Hypothetically it could be argued that it suits capitalism in a time of crisis to educate students in higher education in the most abstruse academic subjects so that on graduation they, along with other sections of the labour force, are unemployed. Equally employers may demand that the most narrow vocational studies are pursued. Yet most employers now realise that their employees require some degree of broader education and not merely acquired skills—in order that they can adapt to changing circumstances of employment. In recognising this, though, they can calculate that it is more profitable to have trained manpower that becomes obsolescent in a relatively short period and employ newer labour later on—thus rendering older workers redundant (cf. the position of teacher wastage mentioned earlier). Of one thing we can be certain—profit comes first.

The conclusion of all this is that the interests of business and employers are catered for in diverse ways—by governments, the DES, Tory LEA's and directly by themselves. Their needs and influence pervade all of higher education, but these interests are sometimes contradictory and often varied and changing. Their position is buttressed by the ideology of capitalist society, and is assumed to be "indispensable", "neutral", "in the national interest" and so on. Everything possible is done to obscure and confuse the basic principle of private profit for the capitalist. Their interests are incorporated within the ideas conventionally purveyed by the media and those which are dominant in society in general. These same ideas themselves commonly underpin school and college curricula. What should students do in this connexion? What should student unions fight for? The Scylla of academicism and the Charybdis of vocationalism are to be avoided.

Courses should be flexible and allow for student choice. Though the influences of business and employers are pervasive they are certainly not all-powerful. Students, teachers and the colleges have an area of autonomy which should be ascertained and used to enable the student to be fully educated and given the maximum choice about what she does on leaving college.

## The 1972 White Paper and the future

Reference has been made on many occasions to the 1972 Tory White Paper on educational priorities now so zealously advocated by Messrs. Prentice and Fowler. It is here intended to summarise the likely effects for higher education. One of the major decisions was to reduce the annual rate of expansion of educational expenditure for the forthcoming decade as compared to 1960–70, by $6\frac{1}{2}$ to 5 per cent. This figure has itself probably become an overestimate because of the cuts in public expenditure announced in December 1973. Many existing capital projects have been deferred and student numbers targets revised downwards. The effects of inflation will barely be met.

The main new policy principle of the White Paper is the divisive pitting of one sector of the education system against others. So Mrs. Thatcher found it necessary to take money from higher education, postgraduate studies in particular, in order to finance an expansion of nursery education. Not only is such a policy morally objectionable, but also it is folly because the education system needs to be developed as a balanced whole if the constituent parts are to function properly. In particular Mrs. Thatcher's nursery school priority No. 1 will require better trained and educated teachers. It will be most difficult for this to be achieved with a reduction in teacher supply targets of 50 per cent over the next decade. In general the problems of the teaching profession will be made worse by a reduced teacher supply despite a lowering of the birth rate (the dubious rationale of Government policy). With the present wastage and drift from the profession it is clear that the pressing present and future educational needs of the schools—curriculum change, reduced class sizes, secondary reorganisation among others —will not be met. The only sop offered to the teaching profession is an expanded programme of in-service training (one term in seven years), which is itself inadequate and will probably not be met in the present crisis of public expenditure.

The Diploma in Higher Education is conceived by the White Paper as an innovation to meet the demands of future generations of school leavers. This will be a two-year course with an "A" level entry requirement and possible eligibility for mandatory award. The reality will be higher education on the cheap. For many on the Dip.HE. it will prove to be a terminal qualification and a substitute for the present three years of a degree or diploma course. Particularly obnoxious is the insistence on the two "A" levels entry requirement. This will restrict access to certain sorts of people—those having just left sixth form as opposed to more mature entrants, who are less likely to have or be inclined to take "A" levels. The qualification will not be particularly marketable and the universities in particular are not likely to give it a full two for two (year) equivalence in the case of students wishing to transfer on to degree courses. This will assist the universities to be more selective. Without full equivalence many will not obtain degrees because grants will only be available for three years.

Student numbers, assessed at 750,000 for 1981, will in all likelihood be quite inadequate, and will not be met because of insufficient finance. The Committee of Polytechnic Directors has recently stated that the student numbers target for that sector will have to be reduced by 40,000 over the next seven or eight years. It is becoming increasingly clear that access to higher and further education is intended to become more difficult as the decade proceeds. This situation may be buttressed by declining levels of student grants and the possibility of some form of student loans. A worsening situation of student support will prevent an increasingly large section of young people, particularly those of working-class backgrounds, getting to college or university.

Compared with the situation a decade ago the colleges and universities will fare badly. There will be less money, more competition for what is available and the corollary of greater Government control about what is done, particularly in the area of innovation. Staffing standards will be reduced as the White Paper norm of 10 : 1 SSR is introduced in all sectors. Fewer staff will mean more lectures, less tutorials and experiment and a greater rigidity of courses. Postgraduate opportunities will be greatly reduced, itself harmfully affecting the teaching intake for higher education.

The outlook is bleak and getting bleaker. Only a government prepared to reverse the disastrous Tory and present Labour record, increase expenditure and raise the student numbers target will provide the answer. Regardless of the short-term needs of the Government or the monopolies it is emphatically in the interests of the British people as a whole that their skills and abilities should be developed to the maximum. The wealth of the country and its social and economic progress ultimately rest on the skills and knowledge of the people. The interests of students here have a far wider significance.

# 2

## THE CIRCUMSTANCES OF STUDENTS

Just as it is necessary to understand the character and development of the higher and further education system, so it is vital to be familiar with the circumstances of students if the student movement is to be appreciated. What follows is an account of the important aspects of the situation in which students find themselves: finance, living conditions, welfare, institutional and educational problems. It is important to realise that student conditions in general have deteriorated in the last decade. At the same time there have been a number of positive changes as a result of student pressure. For the future much will depend on the extent to which the student movement and its allies are able to campaign effectively for reforms. Without the sternest opposition, Tory policies so far mapped out will lead to a worsening of the situation in years to come. In the course of considering students' problems it is necessary to make some mention of student reactions, policies and proposals for change. Chapter 6 pursues this aspect in detail.

### Student finance

Student grants are rightly the best known and most publicised aspect of the student condition. It is abundantly clear that student grants have deteriorated in every respect over the last decade. Despite the fact that the number of student awards made has increased rapidly in recent years, a point governments have often congratulated themselves about, the amount of money in real terms spent on each student has declined. Although Ministers have never admitted it, the decline in value of student awards has resulted in a substantial cash saving. It can only be assumed that this has been a deliberate act of policy. For the student movement the grants issue has three essential features. First, every student suffers in some way and is capable of being mobilised into action around demands for change. Second, the level of grants is a crucial factor bearing on educational opportunity. Inadequate grant levels will act as a disincentive to access to higher and further education—a barrier most particularly for working-class young people and those whose parents are unwilling or unable to provide a substantial subsidy. Third, it is the issue in recent years which has enabled students most effectively to identify with other sections of the population.

The grants system can be seen to be based on a number of principles. These are:

1. The principle of parental dependence or the means test. Students in higher education are legally adults, but for the purpose of student finance this is conveniently forgotten. All but the poorest parents are supposed, but not obliged, to make a contribution according to their income which brings up the level of grant to the full rate. In practice students have the level of their grants reduced, for parents do not always (understandably) pay the contribution. Students can be subject in this situation to an additional reimposed parental authority. Meanwhile the Government saves money. Indeed, so anxious is the Government to save money that in official statistics of expenditure on student awards tuition fees, parental contributions, fees of direct grant and public schools paid by the DES and one or two other items are included. A large and increasing proportion of the student grants budget is theoretical in that it never reaches the students' pocket because of parental non-payment of the contribution.

2. The principle that "to him that hath shall be given" (up to the age of 21). If you are not studying on a first degree or equivalent course—at either postgraduate or sub-degree level—or if you are studying part-time, you have no right at all to student support. It is only for degree and equivalent-level courses that the student has a right to a grant when accepted on to the course. Postgraduate grants have decreased sharply in quantity relative to the numbers of students wishing to undertake postgraduate study. A few say that there should be a system of postgraduate loans. Governments have avoided the political furore this would create by saving the money that loans would bring by reducing the number of grants available. For the student at technical college studying for ONC, City and Guilds qualifications, etc., it is for the individual LEA to decide whether the student is worthy of support—and if so, at what level. It is invidious that degree course students should be valued more highly than others, and that some students should be better treated according to where they live and which

LEA maintains them. Perhaps most obnoxious of all is the fact that a full-time degree course student is supported, but a part-time student on the same course is not. The grant system is still geared to the high academic performance grammar and public school sixth forms, and successful entrants to university and advanced courses. Those who have succeeded have more provision allocated to them than those who have not or those who are trying to.

3. The principle of vacation work. The original justification for vacations was that they allowed the student to study on his own account. Now, the purpose of the vacation is to enable students to earn money to live during the vacations *and* partially finance themselves in term time. The alternatives of bank loans, grinding poverty or substantial parental support are not real options for any but a very small minority.

4. The principle of declining value. By convention the 1962 levels of the main rates of grant are regarded as a reasonable level of student subsistence. Since that time their real value has declined by more than a quarter. In the summer of 1973 the Government took the unprecedented step of making an interim increase to grant levels (one taking place outside the triennial cycle). They were forced to do this by the drastically declining level of grants and the campaign waged by the NUS. Not only are students beaten by inflation, but also the increases conceded are always three years late—another way the Government is able to save money. For students on lower level courses the situation is often worse still. The LEA's can decide their own (lower) level. There are few items of educational expenditure which are directly under the control of the LEA (as opposed to those dictated by statutory requirement). So the numbers and level of discretionary awards can be subjected to a double squeeze in times of restriction on public spending.

5. The principle of sexual discrimination. One of the most blatant examples of sexual discrimination in higher and further education is built into the grants system. If you are a married man the maximum grant you can receive (1974) is £605. If you are a married woman student the maximum grant you can receive regardless of the husband's income is £475. Although between 1965 and 1973 the level of this grant

was fixed at £275, indicating recent improvement, this grant is means-tested against the husband's income. Unlike the situation for men it is assumed that women as adults are not financially independent. Married women are being forced to be increasingly dependent financially on their husbands.

6. The pocket money principle. If you are a student in residence or approved lodgings at a college of education in England or Wales (the situation is different in Scotland), a special low rate of grant is paid. The cost of board and lodging is deducted and the student receives the remainder. Thus unlike their fellow students at polytechnic or university, college of education students do not have full control over the spending of their grant. This is an effrontery to student rights and has long been opposed. It is all the more objectionable because the practice takes place only in teacher education establishments. One can only assume that the rationale is that if student teachers are treated like children they will themselves treat children more like children when they become teachers!

There are many other specific problems caused by the grants system. London postgraduate students do not have a London weighting, unlike undergraduates and many others working in the capital. Specialist groups of students, for example physical education students, do not get enough in their grant to meet the full cost of special equipment that they have to purchase. Vacation grants are now given in a very parsimonious manner by college authorities, thus preventing many who wish to study in the vacations from doing so. Sandwich course students have their own special problems which result in their being underfinanced on industrial placement. All this amounts to a first class educational scandal. Far from it being the case, as has commonly been asserted in the press and by those who don't like students, that students waste public money, in fact every effort is made to minimise what they spend and keep grants as low as possible.

From time to time the question of student loans is raised. Here the student by one of several means would pay back to the state all or part of the cost of his maintenance (and possibly tuition fees too). This would make the present problems of student finance even more acute. Many would find the price charged for higher education prohibitive. Whatever can be said about the exact mechanisms and their educational effects, loans are a means by which the costs of higher education are decisively shifted on to the consumer, the student. Thus they would penalise those who cannot afford the entry charge, whereas the rich parent will always be able to give money to his children and thus obviate the need for a loan and its repayment. Any government introducing loans would be aiming not only at saving money but also at reducing access to higher education.

With about the same regularity the proposal that students should be disciplined by having their grants withdrawn is raised from Tory quarters. Students have vigorously resisted such proposals while college authorities too have opposed the removal of their power of academic assessment. At present an LEA can only cease payment if the college authority so recommends.

## Student housing

Regularly at the beginning of each academic year there is a well-publicised student accommodation crisis. The new students are fitted in somehow. Just as regularly we are told that higher education cannot go on expanding as there will be nowhere for the students to live—unless they live at home in greater numbers. There is a chronic student housing crisis. Not enough places for students to live in, too many places of poor standard, an inadequate programme of residence construction and rents that are too high. The Government and local authorities have not measured up to the task of providing student accommodation cheaply and in sufficient quantity. In 1963 the Robbins Committee recommended that two-thirds of the new students in its expansion programme should be catered for in halls of residence. The Robbins student numbers targets have been well exceeded and far less than two-thirds have been provided for in this way: 40 per cent of new students at university, 12 per cent in colleges of education and 10 per cent in polytechnics, making an overall proportion of 24 per cent, have been so accommodated. Governments have sought to fill the gap by a scheme of loan-financed accommodation in the university sector and a totally inadequate programme of construction in the polytechnics and colleges.

Loan-financed construction means that instead of the old 100 per cent grant system the University Grants Committee will now only meet costs up to rather more than one-quarter of the cost per student place (though with the costs in the capital expenditure the amount of money the UGC has for this purpose is virtually nil). For the rest universities have to borrow capital on the money market at high rates of interest. Local authorities face the same problem and for the same reason. High fees are the result. This combined with paternalistic regulations has led an increasing proportion of students to question the suitability of hall living. Empty places have now appeared in some universities where alternative suitably priced accommodation can be found. At other universities some halls are effectively becoming clubs for the richer students, other students being made to pay the fees.

Students are one of the main sections of the population seeking lodging and flats in the private rented sector. Like everyone else they were forced to pay escalating rents as a result of the Tory Housing Finance Act (1972). Increasingly, students are having to compete with poorer sections and are to some extent displacing the larger and poorer families by their ability to "club together" and multi-occupy. However, the situation for all in this sector is worsening. Although students are eligible for rent rebates and rent allowances under the Housing Finance Act, authorities have discretion in giving them to residents under 30 years of age. The assessment made also includes the parental contribution, whether or not the student actually receives it.

Broadly speaking three solutions or part solutions are offered to solve the student housing problem (apart from a policy of reducing student numbers). Sir William Alexander and a number of influential bodies and individuals have recommended regionalisation of intake. This would mean an increased proportion of students living at home with their parents. Students have always opposed this, as have college authorities with some equivocation. It would limit the student's right to choose where, and incidentally, what to study. Regionalisation would reduce the course options open to applicants and be a severe reduction of educational opportunity for those not living in the south-east, where there is a heavy concentration of population and a very wide range of educational provision to choose from. It would also harmfully affect the institutions themselves, many of which have recently been developed as *national* institutions with a *national* student intake. Given that there is already a substantial number of residence places, regionalisation could only be partial and there would be considerable arbitrariness in deciding who was to be "regionalised" and who could apply where they liked.

Being forced to live at home can reinforce social pressures which are objectionable to the student and cause a greater strain in parent-student relations; physically small homes can make study difficult. There is now a part of the UCCA form for the university applicant to indicate whether he or she is prepared to live at home. Although there is no compulsion this raises the question in a way that was not the case previously.

From time to time some sections of student opinion decide that the way to solve the student housing problem is by self-help methods —student owned and controlled housing, in the form of housing associations or co-operatives. Housing associations sponsored by students and college authorities exist in a number of places. They provide satisfactory accommodation. In a more ambitious way Student Co-operative Dwellings has for some years campaigned for the setting up of student co-operatives to run housing. They have been influenced by student housing in Scandinavia where virtually all student residences are student owned. Recently, in south-east London, Student Co-operative Dwellings has started a housing project. Whilst these particular developments may assist in a limited way they cannot be seen as a substitute for the essential role of public authorities in financing and planning development.

The housing needs of the student body cannot be seen in isolation from the housing needs of the population as a whole. The government and local authorities choose to ignore reality and instead see students in isolation. In 1967 the Building Research Station (under the aegis of the Ministry of Technology) published a paper which showed that student needs were much the same as those of a sizeable proportion of the young people. Since that time it has been a byword of progressive thinking in the student housing field to agree with this and state axiomatically that student housing should be planned for alongside that of others of the same age. Mr. Edward Simpson, Under Secretary of State of the DES, and responsible for higher education, on May 22nd, 1973, said: "A student perhaps married and content to live down town at a lower standard than in a residence hall is very little different in his demands from a young man or woman in employment. There is an artificiality in discussing residence for students, as though they were unique. But if they move out into the town, who are they displacing? Local Authorities will have to pay attention if students take over the one-room or two-room flats formerly occupied by ill-paid families, for example." Quite so. He then said, talking of the DES—"We see the question here but not the answers." Yet the DES caters for student housing in isolation (residence construction in colleges and universities) while the Department of the Environment caters for the housing of the rest of the population. Aren't government departments supposed to provide answers? In order to prevent the situation getting worse, more money will have to be spent by public authorities on student housing and housing in general, but above all else there is a need first to plan for the real situation, not the unreal one of students in isolation.

### Student counselling and graduate unemployment

"Successful suicide and acts of self-injury or poisoning are both more common among students than among others. The national rate for the age group runs at about four per 100,000 per year. Figures from universities are extremely variable, but the redbrick and older universities report rates about three to five times higher, while Oxford and Cambridge have rates nearly seven to ten times higher than this figure . . . one can point to the various stresses of student life, to the high proportion of overseas and hence uprooted people, to examinations, to the loss of status involved in failure and to the fragmented and isolated social circumstances of many students" (Anthony Ryle—*Student Casualties*, 1969).

Nicholas Malleson of the London University sponsored Educational Redeployment Service, an agency designed to help students who wish to change courses, has estimated that 15 per cent of the student body are at risk of some form of nervous disorder during their course.

These figures indicate that insufficient is done to assist students in difficulty and to provide the right level of advice and counselling to all students. The problems of Oxbridge are worse than at other universities despite the fact that these institutions have traditionally based their education on a collegiate system and one-to-one tutorials. This shows the need for a fully professional advice system, as opposed to the amateur "don counsellor" (though the high status of Oxbridge and the high expectations placed on students there, makes for greater "pressures" than elsewhere). In further education colleges in particular there is still a prevalent "hail fellow well met" attitude, an antiquated

Boy Scout approach, which is of quite inadequate assistance for students. There is a need for a greater professionalism and co-ordination between different agencies—those responsible for careers guidance, for medical and counselling services and those working in different institutions of higher education. At the same time it must be recognised that part of the cause of the personal problems that students face are educational and social in nature. It is necessary to remove the causes—over-specialisation at school, rigid time-test examinations, graduate unemployment, etc. Counselling cannot remove these problems.

In recent years there has been a growing concern about the problem of graduate unemployment and underemployment. This has prompted amongst some a more critical concern with the purposes of higher education. There is evidence indicating that the problem has lessened somewhat in the last year or two. In 1972 the UGC's First Employment of University Graduates indicated that 7·8 per cent were still seeking employment on December 31st and that 10·1 per cent were of unknown destination. In 1965 the respective percentages were 2·3 and 4·7. Some have concluded from this that there are too many students or that the courses being studied are not sufficiently vocational. There is a deceptive plausibility about both of these assertions. Cutting student numbers would reduce graduate unemployment. But it would not reduce unemployment in general, merely change its designation. The causes of graduate unemployment are basically the same as those for unemployment as a whole—deflationary Government policies, inadequate investment in British industry and slow rate of economic growth. Indeed, it is generally accepted that education, however vocational or academic, is an asset in seeking employment. Though even if it were not, this would not in itself be sufficient reason for curtailing the numbers of students, as education is concerned with more than preparation for employment. The second proposition is equally specious. Although some employers will say that graduates are not specialised enough or sufficiently practical in their outlook, technological and social change dictates that a high importance be attached to an ability to think clearly and to innovate. Both measures are self-contradictory and highly damaging to student interests.

Graduates today cannot expect to have the same status or remuneration in employment that their predecessors had ten or fifteen years ago. Starting salaries for many graduates are little above those of non-graduates, and often significantly below average industrial earnings, e.g., teaching. Although employers have wanted increased numbers of skilled workers, they have not required proportionately more people in highly paid and high status positions. The greater competition now means that many are not "successful". Higher education has come to resemble the position of secondary and grammar school education before the 1944 Education Act. For students trained to have high expectations the result has been a disillusionment about the economic advantages of a higher education and a recognition that graduate status is not what it was. Employment problems now facing students increasingly resemble those faced by large sections of the population.

### Student representation

Historically the issue of representation, that students should be represented on major decision-making committees, and the wider matter of democratisation, have been very important in the development of the student movement. Although there is mention of democratisation in NUS documents produced as early as 1940, it was not until the 1960's that ideas on representation became clarified. In October 1966 the NUS produced *Student Representation in College Government*. This followed experience with the charters of new universities where the Privy Council was anxious to ensure that student representation was ineffective. The Weaver Report on the government of colleges of education published in 1966 led to reforms in this sector, though it made no explicit mention of student representation. In 1967–8 the main push for representation took place over the articles of government of the polytechnics.

In the six or seven years since that time a number of tangible successes have been achieved. It is now accepted by college authorities and the DES that student representation has a role in institutional government. This was not the position in the mid 1960's. Student representation now exists in all institutions of higher education and a large number of colleges of further education. This representation has been used to positive effect in many instances to carry forward policies of benefit to students (a particularly good example is the Polytechnic of North London where student votes on both the Court of Governors and the academic board have on a number of occasions had an important effect in determining the course of events). On the other hand it is abundantly clear that representation has weaknesses. The main ones are: that on many occasions students have been easily outvoted on important decisions; that important decisions can be taken by bodies where students are unrepresented or by informal caucus; that student representatives do not have equivalent status to other members of a committee, e.g., they may not have votes or may only attend when asked by the committee; that student unions have often seen representation as an end in itself rather than a means of securing changes benefiting students; that the practice of reserved areas has been applied systematically—important items of business are denied the attention of students, e.g., staff appointments. The college and university authorities now use more subtle techniques to limit student representation. It is no longer politic for them to confront it head on—why not try *divide et impera* by buying off and deceiving the union leadership with token representation? For example, two recent reports of enquiry into universities—the Grimond Review Body at Birmingham and the Murray Enquiry for London—both recommended an extension of student representation, but they were careful to avoid recommending any increase on the most important decision-making bodies.

## Student discipline

Student discipline, regulations of student conduct and their enforcement by college authorities have all been very important and highly sensitive matters in recent years. In former times college authorities were often able to punish students with impunity—there would be little chance of adverse student reaction. The overwhelming majority of students accepted without question both the aims and purposes of the institution and the right of the authorities to apply discipline as they saw fit. They claimed to be *in loco parentis*. Changes in student attitudes towards the colleges and universities, deeper movements in social values, the lowering of the age of majority to 18 (though for the purposes of student grants the individual is not assumed to be independent, i.e. an adult, unless three years of paid employment has been completed before study or the person is over 25 years of age), and an earlier maturation to adulthood, have altered the situation profoundly. Proper and due procedures of discipline have had to be established. No longer can the authorities exercise the same discretion.

The most offensive aspects of older disciplinary practice were fourfold:

1. The *in loco parentis* philosophy which prevents students behaving in an adult manner.

2. The practice of double discipline, which allows the college authority to try a student for an offence in addition to any proceedings instigated by the civil authorities.

3. The exercise of summary powers—allowing Vice-Chancellors and Principals to act in an authoritarian and headmasterly fashion.

4. The "bringing the name of the college into disrepute" rule, often applied with 3. This vague and often vacuous charge has caused many problems, though since 1969, with the Hart Report—Committee on Relations with Junior Members, at Oxford—it has fallen into decline.

Pettiness and heavy handedness have often made these grievances worse. Students have fought all four with some success and, although problems of discipline remain, they do so in smaller measure. A more adult atmosphere prevails, double discipline is less likely and summary powers are now more clearly circumscribed.

Part of the grievance about discipline has always been procedural, that cases have been badly and unjustly handled. In this area the objective has been to secure the adoption of the principles of a "fair hearing"—the right of representation, the right of appeal to a separate body, the rights of being able to bring forward witnesses and to cross-examine, the keeping of a written record and the student being informed of his offence in writing. These principles have been largely won, although in the difficult borderline area between academic and non-academic offences authorities have been able to get round them.

Concern over procedural matters and the questions of double discipline, *in loco parentis*, etc., has tended to leave an important area ignored. This is the substance of college regulations and the extent to which an institution should have any regulations at all, apart from those relating to the admission, assessment and certification of students. Some debate has taken place, and hall regulations together with the more petty rules have been challenged. Yet many dubious regulations still exist in many colleges. Unless the substance of regulations and rules are appreciated student representation on disciplinary committees can be a major problem. There is little point in student representatives helping to implement regulations opposed to student interests.

Some have argued that there should be no regulations at all, apart from those concerned with academic questions. The rules and laws of society should apply on the campus, the argument runs, and if these are deemed unsatisfactory it would be incumbent on students to change the laws of society. There are a number of powerful arguments in support of this contention. On the one hand students do not need "protecting" from the law and on the other they must on no account be subject to double discipline. The special regulations of the college or university also demonstrate the isolated nature of the institutions of higher education, their essential lack of concern for the problems of the community. Student opinion on this matter has vacillated, particularly when the police have come on to campus. Such developments have usually been met with the demand "pigs off the campus". Yet at Stirling in the disciplining of Linda Quinn, President of the Students Association, an argument often used by the students was that she would never have been tried, let alone found guilty of the offences charged by the university, in a court of law.

The best way of dealing with this problem is to apply the premise that a community has the right to decide in a democratic manner how it wishes to regulate its own conduct and the behaviour of its members—with due regard to personal freedom and the wider laws of society. Second, no one can seriously challenge the right of a college to apply library rules and similar regulations covering day to day matters. Such matters are properly outside the realm of public law. Third, the college must not stand, or be seen to stand, in moral judgement over students' behaviour. This applies to personal questions over which the college has no responsibility and to wider issues of social philosophy. Finally, it must be a matter of policy for the colleges to minimise and simplify their regulations in the non-academic area and to ensure that they do not clash with or attempt to override or supplement the laws of society in general.

Another approach has been to get the colleges and universities to be much more specific and open about the regulations that do exist and to set these out in the form of a contract which the student would have to sign on admission to the college. This approach was recommended by the ill-fated "Academic Freedom and the Law" report in 1971. Though argued with the best of intentions it was rejected widely in the student body because it was felt that a "campus contract" would be more advantageous to college authorities than to students. It resembled too closely the *carte blanche* "good behaviour pledge" that students have from time to time been threatened with.

Despite the progress made, many disciplinary codes and procedures remain unsatisfactory. And the victimisation of student union officers will increase if, as seems likely, they continue to be the representatives of militant policies. College authorities feel most strongly that officers of unions should not be allowed "immunity" from university and college regulations. Complaints about "being above the law" are out of place, for the issue is not the misdemeanours of particular individuals, but rather the right of the student body collectively to instruct its elected officers without fear of their being punished for carrying out their democratic duties. It is not the job of union officers to be "responsible" as far as the authorities are concerned, to do their job for them. Such disciplinary action strikes at the principle of union autonomy and democracy. In the context of future disputes we can anticipate some outraged liberal turned reactionary Vice-Chancellor (as opposed to the more traditional and now less common dyed-in-the-wool type), trying to exercise summary powers, or a "liberal and modern" disciplinary code being used against elected student officers. Proctors, too, continue to exist at Oxford and Cambridge. Academics turned policemen dressed in rather quaint clothes may attract tourists to these seats of learning in the summer, but they must go. It will be a great victory for the student movement as a whole when these two universities finally bring themselves out of their medieval past.

## Student assessment

The most powerful way in which students' behaviour is controlled is through the examination system. Widespread concern and opposition has been expressed by students to the traditional pattern of exams. In some areas definite reforms have been gained. Educational opinion and teacher opinion in particular has moved against examinations as the sole or even the most substantial form of assessment.

In 1967–8 radicals such as Charles Wright, Tom Fawthrop and Leo Smith stated the view that exams were the primary mechanism by which the universities and colleges controlled students and that grading was the means by which the institutions provided society and employers with the different varieties of "product" they required. Students were prepared for their roles as employees by examinations inculcating the appropriate submissive attitudes. The whole set-up was styled the "degree factory". Examinations are a means of control in that their finality concentrates the student's mind on the performance of the desired tasks. They induce a competitive spirit amongst students and play on the fear of failure. Their apparent objectivity, and the belief by students in this, acts as a powerful justification for many students. As Charles Wright said: "He is completely subjected to the will of others, though the human nature of this domination is disguised by its apparent impersonality and objectivity." However, student attitudes to examinations are ambiguous. Students are experienced and successful at passing them. They are reassuring to those who do not want the challenge of educational innovation and a more self-directed pattern of study. Some students even feel that under a more liberal regime they would not do so well.

In the last six years the weight of opinion and argument against examinations has increased considerably. In particular "A" level entry requirements are progressively creating an 11-plus type selection in access to higher education. For some time the Schools Council and the Standing Conference on University Entrance has been investigating possibilities for reform. Yet all this has come to very little. No agreement has been reached and the increasingly discredited "A" levels look like being with the schools and the students for a long time to come. Mr. Short, when Secretary of State, said, "The examination is, I often think, a great disincentive to true education. The traditional examination which still hangs round the neck of the schools, tests what it tests and nothing more." He went on to argue for a profile-cum-continuous-assessment system to be adopted in the schools. While it is fine to have influential friends on matters like these, action is what counts.

Despite the fact that some reforms in examinations have been made by individual universities and the CNAA, they still form the central feature of assessment in higher education. This position must be attacked, for exams are not a reliable way of assessing students. It has been shown that the results gained depend upon the mood and opinion of the examiner, the number of times the scripts are read and the number of examiners, the ability of students to stand up to strain, good examination technique, luck and question-spotting by the students, normal variations in performance by students from time to time and the choice of the right question by the student. There is some evidence to suggest that examinations are a strong causative factor in the psychological illnesses that some students suffer from. They prevent much useful educational work being done in the third term of the academic year. They can cause an artificially narrowed curriculum, the set syllabus being dominant in the student's mind. Teachers will advise and students accept that there is little point in studying outside the syllabus because no questions on such material will appear in the examination.

Examinations must be seen, moreover, in association with the other two major traditional features of British universities and the education system in general—the excessive use of the lecture as a teaching method and artificially defined academic subject boundaries. Together they prevent students seeing the full interrelationships between different areas of knowledge and human activity. This "holy trinity" is the educational basis of much of current student discontent with their courses. Examinations are the most obvious and objectionable part. Above all they can be very unfair to students. Some perform well under examination conditions, others do not. They may, if the student does well in examinations, test the educational attainment of the student. If the student does not, they will test whether the student is good at rote learning and recall, whether he can write essays and write them quickly, and whether he can question-spot.

An essential feature of the examination system is grading. Examinations would lose much of their potency as an incentive to student study if there was not the possibility of getting a first or an upper second-class degree. The usual justification for grading is that employers and society in general need to know how good someone is. This ignores the following points:

1. Most employers are not concerned with the precise degree

grading. They want to know little more than whether someone has a degree or not. Except in recruitment to specialised posts, e.g. a research chemist, employers consider that they can decide better than the colleges and universities whether an applicant is suitable.

2.  The major reason for grading is that the institution needs to carry it out for its own purposes—as a justification, and as a means of providing information which will be relevant in making a decision about someone's suitability for a further course. Grading clearly defines those who are best suited for acceptance into research and higher study—an initiation process.

3. Examinations cannot predict future performance in the educational or employment contexts. At best all they can do is to say that a student can do certain sorts of things (or not) at a specific time. Primarily they indicate something about the past activities of the student and in particular whether he has learnt to be proficient at exam taking.

4. Grading students is not dissimilar from streaming them. Streaming in any educational context makes it less likely that pupils will behave in a way unsuitable for the particular stream—the self-fulfilling prophecy.

5.  Above all else a grade is a relative assessment. There can be no qualitative distinction between someone who just fails to get an upper second degree and another who just succeeds in so doing.

In short assessment is in need of radical reform. Students must be fully involved in the process of devising and framing reforms.

*General educational matters*

Despite the rapid expansion of the colleges and universities in the last decade there has been no general improvement in the facilities of study available to students. Whilst libraries are larger and there is more academic accommodation, the number of students using what is available has increased relative to this. The DES and Local Education Authorities have been anxious to ensure the most economic possible use of "plant". Of particular educational importance is the intention to raise the average staff-student ratio, especially in the university sector. No amount of efficient planning can make the proverbial butter spread more thinly. There will be some serious effects for teaching methods. Fewer staff, less money for teaching aids, less opportunities for secondments and in service training will mean a regression to older and discredited practices. The choice may be between being over-lectured or being under-lectured with little other contact with staff.

There is now a greater range of educational options and types of courses available than ever before. However, the main problem with many of the new courses has been to secure an interaction between different areas of study. Staff educated on single-subject highly specialised honours degrees are ill equipped to teach in new ways. The result has been that some courses under the most liberal guise are best described as abortive, where students study separate, disparate or divergent subjects and are themselves expected to produce on their own the desired synthesis. In this situation students are the victims of someone else's ill-conceived educational experiment and are rightly angry.

Another major area of development has been sandwich courses, particularly in the technological universities and polytechnics. These have received considerable support from the Government, LEA's and to a lesser extent, the employers. Undoubtedly they are suitable for the student who wants a clearly defined career. However, they have thrown up a number of major problems. They can be inflexible in that the objective is to prepare the student for a particular type of employment exemplified by the placement. Unemployment or total misemployment has resulted from overall economic factors, there being insufficient placements available in a time of recession. The courses tend to be illiberal and narrow. Accordingly, the student on a sandwich course may be in a "rut" he is unable to get out of, like the student on the single-subject honours degree course.

One of the most important changes in recent years has been the move towards unit course structures. They have provided students with a wider range of choices, but have shown up the weaknesses that exist on the counselling side. Unit based courses were first attempted in a substantial way in this country by the Open University. Courses are broken down into a number of discrete parts or units. The student requires unit total in order to pass a degree and he obtains this by selecting the self-contained options and "building" his own course. The idea is to provide for an *à la carte* type course, as opposed to the traditional *table d'hôte*, variety. In principle this is a better arrangement, but it requires excellent academic organisation, very good counselling and imaginative curricular planning. Otherwise the student can merely dabble in a number of diverse areas and finish his studies confused, disoriented and dissatisfied. With the straight-through type of course it is easier to engender a social and participatory atmosphere because the student is in one department for most of the course. The problem with unit courses is that the role of the student as consumer can be emphasised to the detriment of his being an active participant in the planning and development of courses. He "shops in the supermarket" while the management decides the range of "goods", paying some attention to consumer demand. In order to prevent the atomisation of the student body it is essential that there should be a democratic academic structure and a strong union able to draw the students together and articulate their views. The student must also have a core or theme to his studies to which he relates his choice of units and balance of studies.

Notwithstanding these three developments the main problem of British higher education remains over-specialisation. Educational choices taken at fourteen or fifteen still decide the career a graduate will enter eight years later. This was recognised as harmful by the Dainton and Macarthy reports in 1968. The remedy is to be found in reducing the subject emphasis of secondary and post-school education and making it more activity and project oriented. Certainly, improving the possibilities for transfer by the use of bridging and foundation courses and other devices is essential. Over-specialisation is harmful from every point of view. The student decides his career or occupation on what can be an immature judgement. As a result employers have to employ people who may not be fully committed to their jobs. The restrictive effect of over-specialisation is most clearly seen in the teaching profession where it is reinforced by the institutional, social and financial isolation of the colleges of education. Reluctant or unthinking teachers make bad teachers, and teacher wastage benefits no one.

By tradition and convention the curriculum is not central in public educational debate in this country. Education is in large measure seen as numbers, structures and costs. The main reason for this is that decisions about the curriculum are a matter for teachers (heads of department) and academics (professors). Challenges to the curriculum become awkward challenges to professional competence. Academic freedom for academics and the due prerogative of the teaching profession take the curriculum out of the political sphere. For the ruling class this has advantages and disadvantages. On the one hand it is not possible to control directly what is going on in the schools and colleges, i.e. there is a certain risk. On the other, this delegation ensures that the actual political and ideological content of curricula are obscured and as a rule unchallenged. In this last connexion the recent increased concern with the curriculum on the part of left-wing students and teachers is to be welcomed.

Curricula in English education pose a number of problems. The delegation of authority to an institution and its staff (as opposed to ministerial control in France) means that there is a bewildering variety of curricula despite external moderation, inspection and even examination.

It is practically possible for left-wing students and teachers to function with a substantial measure of independence (this notwithstanding the witch hunts on left staff in recent years—Craig at Lancaster, Atkinson at Birmingham and Blackburn at the LSE). Second, it is practically very difficult for student unions and the NUS to organise activities on curricular questions, except perhaps on isolated issues. The strategic approach has always been to leave the initiative to individuals and small groups. The extent of variety makes even the co-ordination of activities between different groups of students on the same course in different institutions difficult. In addition, the curriculum is a difficult question to get to grips with intellectually. It is much easier for activists to deal with questions of number, structure and cost. Finally, there is little history of student or other radical activity around the curriculum, with the exception of particular issues like careers, peace, trade union studies, black studies in teacher education, etc.

In the French context it is possible to make a frontal attack on curricula for being antiquated, rigid and little related to students' needs. The variety and at least theoretical opportunity for reform makes it difficult to avoid on the one hand the crude view that all education is bourgeois and therefore to be opposed, or on the other to become so involved in the minutiae of departmental affairs so as to lose all wider perspective.

# 3

## THE DEVELOPMENT OF STUDENT UNIONS
## AND THE NATIONAL UNION OF STUDENTS

The student unions and the NUS are the central strength of the student movement. They are stable organisations that have existed for many years catering for a wide variety of student interests and concerns, though at certain times they have been more relevant to the needs and aspirations of some students than of others. Their strength lies in the fact that they are mass, representative organisations providing an opportunity for student self-government, undertaking activities of interest to students and responding to the needs of the diverse sections of the student body. This chapter will outline their history.

### Origins

There have been student clubs and societies for as long as universities and colleges have existed. Some of the ideas which are of immediate and current concern, e.g., representation, have a long history too. In medieval Italian universities a state of "student power" existed, in that students appointed and dismissed staff. However, a century ago in England the student body was largely concentrated at the universities of Oxford and Cambridge and the only manifestations of activity were "horseplay, lightly tinged with politics; a hubbub in the gallery of senate house at congregations or during voting for the high steward; three groans for the proctors and pleasantries howled at distinguished men on ceremonial occasions" (Ashby and Anderson, *The Rise of the Student Estate*).

Yet it was at Oxbridge that student unions in England first appeared, not in their modern form, but as debating societies. At that time it was through debating that a corporate student identity was expressed. The union societies were individual membership organisations which sought to secure some student activity at a level above the individual colleges of the university. Porter Butts expresses it in these terms: "The original idea of the union, essentially, was to form a university-wide society which cut across separate college lines, aiming to achieve some semblance of unity 'through the understanding of differences', through debate and the rivalry and fellowship that went with it. The name 'union' seemed natural because the new organisation 'united' the existing debating societies of the individual colleges. At Oxford, in fact the first name chosen was the 'United Debating Society'" (*Association of College Unions International*, 1967). The union society was formed in 1815 at Cambridge and in 1823 at Oxford. From the outset these were autonomous organisations, quite separate from the universities, unlike modern student unions. Autonomy, then as now, was an important question. Porter Butts records: "In the beginning, the unions met with the active disapproval of the administration, the opposition in part based on the concern that debating would occupy time students should spend studying, and in part on the fear that undesirable results or criticisms might arise from free and open discussion on such a broad scale. The proctor at Cambridge suspended the newly formed union, in 1817, 'because he suspected it of subversive activities'."

These debating unions were of limited scope by modern standards. Indeed, in the modern context their main influence at Oxford, Cambridge and Durham universities is a reactionary one. But they did establish two important principles—autonomy of student organisations and the educational importance of activities undertaken by students themselves. Debating was until quite recently a central activity of all student unions and the Oxbridge pattern was a model for many of the developments that took place in the nineteenth century, e.g., the forming of the Men's Union at Manchester University in 1861 (at this time all unions were fairly strictly segregated between men and women). The debating style unions tended to be little more than rich men's clubs. In 1850 a major Government enquiry (the Clarendon Commission) was established to look into the affairs of Oxford and Cambridge Universities. No student representations were made to it by any local or national student organisation or group. Indeed, the rich men's club idea of unions has always dogged Oxbridge. Student Representative Councils were not established until the 1960's—fifty years behind most other universities.

Towards the end of the nineteenth century the situation began to change. Universities began to assume wider roles; student numbers expanded. They ceased finally to be merely appendages of the Church. In this period debating unions alone proved to be inadequate, and different sorts of organisation began to develop.

It is in Scotland that these changes were first seen. There are a number of reasons for this. There is a closer cultural tie with more continental patterns of higher education. Social access to Scottish universities has always been more broadly based than in English universities. At that time there was a more lively student body than south of the border. The institution of rector has a long history in Scotland and has always been associated with the practice of indirect student representation on the court of the university, the governing body of Scottish universities. In 1860 the students at Marischal College, Aberdeen, were particularly angry about the decision of the Principal of the College to overrule their preference as to who the rector should be. Scottish university student representation until recently has been better than elsewhere. The court of Scottish universities is small in size and a deliberative body, unlike the English university court which is basically a body having ceremonial functions and approving decisions taken elsewhere.

In 1834 at Edinburgh University some student societies decided to associate together. These were the Dialectic, the Scots Law, the Diagnostic, the Hunterian Medical and the Plinian. They formed a body called the Associated Societies, governed by a Council composed of two representatives per society. This is the first historical example of student self-government. A Student Representative Council was formed in 1884. Other Scottish universities soon followed suit. As a result of representations to the Privy Council and other highly placed and influential persons in Scotland the SRC's received full recognition under the Universities (Scotland) Act of 1889. Some of the principles of modern student unionism are clearly inscribed in this Act. The universities are to recognise SRC's as legitimate channels between the student body and the university. Equally important was the recognition that students are *civis universitatis*, that is to say, citizens of the university (see also appendix 4). They were members and this conferred on them certain rights. Edinburgh was then something of an example in student organisation to those elsewhere and it took the initiative in establishing a co-ordinating framework for Scottish SRC's. This ultimately became the Scottish Union of Students in the 1930's.

Little was happening meanwhile at the premier English universities of Oxford and Cambridge. In the 1890's sporadic attempts to form student organisations wider than the single society or social group were attempted at University College London and King's College London.

However, student aspiration sought little more than the occasional magazine and sporting facility. The first SRC in England was formed in the 1890's at Liverpool, then one of the three constituent colleges of the Victoria University. Some conflict with the university surrounded its early development. The next important development was the acceptance of recognition for the first time at an English university in the foundation of the University of Birmingham in 1900. Notional student representation on the court of the university was also conceded. The student organisations recognised were a Guild of Graduates and a Guild of Students. At the time SRC's were little more than a representative framework. The Guilds were the first examples of a modern student union which sought to undertake a number of functions—social, recreational, educational and representational. Following the developments at Birmingham, recognition was conceded at all universities, subsequently awarded charters—most immediately the civic universities of Manchester, Sheffield, Leeds and Liverpool. In 1908 the old Queen's University of Ireland was broken up and the Queen's University of Belfast established. Here a pattern of academic government approximating more to the Scottish pattern was the rule and the new charter allowed for one student representative on the senate.

Since that time all new universities have had student unions established within them as the recognised bodies of communication and representation. The setting up of these unions has enabled the student body nationally to press for advancements which could then serve as models elsewhere. Colleges of education and technical colleges setting up student unions tended to copy the Birmingham Guild model. Of particular note have been the polytechnics, where large, unified and potentially powerful unions now exist, and the new Scottish universities—Stirling, Strathclyde, and Heriot-Watt—where student associations as opposed to SRC's were established. Respectively they served as examples for the public sector in Scotland. The main tendency in the history of the last twenty-five years has been towards amalgamation. Older voluntary membership bodies—sporting clubs and debating unions—have come within the overall union umbrella and received money from student union fee income. In turn the union has obtained this money from the university or college as part of the registration, matriculation or tuition fee. The most recent examples of amalgamation in the university sector have been Newcastle in 1969 and Cambridge, where the Union Society joined the Cambridge Students Union in 1973 (although Cambridge still has no proper students' union).

Ashby and Anderson reviewing the history of the last century attribute the main force for change in student organisation to groups of committed activists and university authorities benevolently accepting their views. The student body as a whole is portrayed as apathetic and disinterested. Whilst the importance of activists and pioneers cannot be denied, a full historical appreciation must take into account all the conditions pertaining at different times. The view that the "student estate" has gradually become better and better largely because of the strivings of dedicated moderate leaders and establishment benevolence does not square with all the facts. Sir Sydney Caine, Director of the LSE until 1967, expressed a rather different view: "I have no doubt that the creation of the modern type of student union was a mistake." The last Tory Government agreed with this and tried to dismantle what had been built.

## The National Union of Students

The NUS has existed continuously since 1922. Formally, its origins antedate the First World War, when the British Universities Congress existed. This embodied two features of importance to the NUS later on—the federal principle and the Congress. There were similar developments in Scotland, though there the conference of SRC's started before the British Universities Congress, and a separate Scottish Union of Students was set up in the 1930's. This eventually petered out, and in 1971 the individual students' unions in Scotland joined up with the NUS.

The original impulse to form a national union rather than a loose co-ordinating framework was provided by the First World War. Such was the revulsion of war and the desire for international understanding that an international conference of students convened in Prague in 1921 founded the Confédération Internationale des Étudiants. The NUS was formed largely to enable British students to be properly represented in the CIE. The first ten years of the Union were difficult ones. Support amongst British students gradually developed, but not without problems, particularly after it became clear that the CIE was not going to be a very effective organisation. At its foundation the NUS established a Travel Department which soon acquired a pre-eminence internationally and an esteem amongst the membership which it still maintains (now as NUS Travel Ltd.). Casework activities and a vacation work department followed in the late 1920's and early 1930's. It was not until some time later that the Union claimed any representative status as far as the Government was concerned. In 1927 the NUS established its first formal relations with the Association of University Teachers.

The NUS made some loans to individual students in the 1930's in order to alleviate hardship, a practice which would not be repeated today. In its first ten years the NUS was by no means radical. Ashby and Anderson writing of the attitude of students to the 1926 General Strike state: "Today a strike of such dimensions would polarise student opinion, with a majority demonstrating in favour of the strikers. In 1926 all those students who took any interest at all helped to break the strike; the handful of students that sympathised with the workers found themselves cold shouldered by their friends, regarded as subversive rebels. The corporate and social conscience of students had not been aroused." The same authors attribute the NUS's survival over the first years in part to good fortune and the dedication of the early leaders like Ivison Macadam, who remains as one of the NUS's Trustees. The journal *Student Vanguard* (March 1934) commented on the atmosphere of an NUS Council: "The Presidents of the Union Societies of England and Wales have recently assembled for a meeting of the Executive Committee of the NUS, which functioned formally in the University of Sheffield and informally in the Grand Hotel. In addition the delegates attended two dinners, a ball and a dance. This was, doubtless, very enjoyable for the guests, but the rank and file of Sheffield may be excused for thinking that the best interests of student intercourse were hardly served by the complete mobilisation of the liquid resources of their Union. The first evening found the delegates sat down with the Master Cutler (the honoured man of Sheffield's armaments manufacturers) and the Chief Constable with the President of the students union to make a speech about the mutual benefits to be derived from a close association between the students, staff and businessmen of Sheffield. The dinner of the second evening was also made the excuse for an unwarranted interference by the home Vice-Chancellor in the form of 'advice' as to what principles should guide delegates in their discussion."

At this time in the Union's history the governing body of the NUS was the Council (it is today called the Conference), which met three times a year. Its basic roles were much the same as at the present day—it elected a National Executive, could not commit the constituent organisations and was the body to which the Executive reported and from which it received its instructions. It was much smaller than the present-day Conference and was dominated by university unions. However, at the time there was another body of considerable importance to the NUS—the Congress. This met annually to discuss the important issues of the day. It aimed at being a mass event, lasting for about a week and provided a focal point for ideas in the student world and for any action which might result. Unlike the Council meetings it was not constitutionally prevented from discussing political questions. The leftward move was representative of students as a whole. A Vice President of the NUS visited Republican Spain and on return toured the colleges and universities to galvanise support; in 1936 there was an NUS contingent on a national peace demonstration; the NUS began to participate in the British Youth Peace Assembly in 1938; in 1940 it produced a document *Defend the Universities* and campaigned against conscription. A document written to commemorate the 21st anniversary of the NUS said; "At last the NUS was seen to be more than an organisational and bureaucratic entity, it was assuming the character of a real student movement, taking its inspiration from the students. The change had been gradual, one taking years of effort, and the importance of Leeds (where the 1940 Congress was held) lay in the fact that it marked the culmination and final achievement of this effort."

As well as becoming a mass movement the NUS developed a more radical educational policy. This is particularly well shown in *A Student's View of the Universities* by Brian Simon, who was NUS President in 1939–40. The following is a sample of what was campaigned for at the time: a single educational code for all children between the ages of 11 and 18, no fees for schooling, compulsory school attendance up to 16, maintenance grants, free school meals, no classes over thirty in number, no uncertificated teachers, health provisions, special schools, the provision of nursery schools, recreational facilities, adequate school buildings and an increase in grants to Local Education Authorities. The Charter adopted at the 1940 Congress has a number of important educational principles, still relevant to the student movement of the present time (appendix 1). Part of this development was the constitutional change in 1937 which allowed teacher training colleges and technical colleges into NUS membership for the first time. It broadened the membership base and made the Union larger and stronger. Prior to this the NUS had been a solely university student organisation. It is interesting to compare the educational policy statements of those times with the present day ones. The similarities are obvious—a radical criticism of the admissions policies of the universities, the objection to narrow and over-specialised courses, a concern for the relevance of studies to society as a whole and a desire for representation in college and university government. However, there are a number of equally obvious differences; the mechanism by which student representation was to be given effect was staff-student consultative committees with administrative powers delegated to them. There was no significant mention of the trade union movement—contact with the people was seen only in a very wide popular sense in the context of the war and the anti-fascist struggle. Concentration on the curriculum was more direct than it is at present. There was no significant policy about the binary system—the future of the training colleges was seen much as the 1944 McNair Report recommended, a close association with the universities. This last point can probably be explained by the fact that the NUS had little membership outside the universities, that student organisation elsewhere was weak and that there was little advanced or degree level work done in the public sector. Students were generally less critical than they are now of the universities and their position within the education system and society in general. The NUS document *The Future of the University and Higher Education in 1944* illustrates this—"it would be impertinent of students to offer any detailed criticism of the present method of selection of university staff".

Outlooks had begun to change in the 'thirties as a result of the wider political situation, though it was not until the end of the decade and the imminence of world war that a student movement of mass proportions began to emerge. The rise of fascism forced students to respond politically, while the economic crisis altered the situation for many graduates. Radicalisation initially involved a minority, but touched wider and wider numbers until the 1940 NUS Congress, a student meeting of mass proportions, when a radical position against the policies of the Chamberlain government was adopted. The students felt particularly annoyed at Lord Halifax's statement that the war was "youth against youth". The prevalent anti-German racial theories of Lord Vansittart were likewise rejected.

During the Second World War the NUS took an active lead in mobilising students for the war effort. Students in some numbers became involved in the defensive activities of the 1940 blitz. A pamphlet *Students and the Blitz* stated: "Reality is a stream in which every academician should receive baptism before he can adequately tackle any job in life. Those of us who went to Stepney at least thrust our big toes into the stream and found it icy. We know what it is like to be bombed out. We know what shelters look and smell like. We have learned a new respect for the capacity of the people to organise themselves to meet emergency with fortitude and intelligence. From us who were briefly a part of this great and terrible experience, must go forth a call to the universities of Britain. The society passing through this ordeal is our society, we must make ourselves ready to play our part." The Union was here clearly identifying with the popular nature of the anti-fascist struggle.

The progressive developments that were at the the time evident in the student body are further brought out by the following extract from the 1942 Congress resolution (which was adopted with 1,155 votes in favour, 9 against and 39 abstentions): "We recognise too that our duties do not end with the war. It is our task, in firm friendship with the freedom-loving students of all countries, to find with the rest of our generation an answer to fascism which will be the foundation for a more just and peaceful world. . . . We reject utterly all theories and actions of race hatred and are convinced that in the occupied territories and in Germany itself we have allies whose heroism and sacrifice show their resolve to join with us in the final destruction of fascism. We believe that the surest answer to the fascist challenge lies in the building of a society which is free from all forms of subjugation and is based on a vital democracy and an economic system in which the resources of the world are used to the full benefit of all. . . ."

One of the most important developments of the war years was the decision to make November 17th International Students Day. On this date in 1939 the Nazis closed the Czechoslovak universities and attacked the student movement. In the autumn of 1941 discussions began in London between the NUS and groups of foreign students living in Britain. The day of solidarity was initiated in this country and observed in the USA, USSR, New Zealand, South America and many other countries. An International Council of Students was formed in Britain at that time, with the NUS President as chairman. It had wide international support and was in some respects the organisational precursor of the IUS.

After the war International Students Day was taken up by the International Union of Students and it campaigns around that day to this date.

At the time the NUS played a leading role in international student affairs. In 1944–5 the great tide of anti-fascist unity led to a conviction that a new international student organisation needed to be created. The International Union of Students was formed in 1946 at a meeting in Prague. The NUS took a leading part in establishing this body, provided the first general secretary (Tom Madden) and largely wrote the constitution and standing orders.

The international commitment to the IUS was a focal point of conflict in the NUS over the next twenty years. By 1948 the cold war was gaining in strength. Intense pressure aimed at splitting the IUS and undermining the progressive leadership of the Union was generated. The leadership began to move to the right from this time onwards, though there was a left-wing minority on the Executive until 1955. The 1949–50 *NUS Yearbook* while complaining of the "partisan" nature of the IUS felt able to say: "The IUS has continued to develop its departments and practical activities. . . . The NUS has continued to send strong delegations to IUS Conferences and Council Meetings." An Associate Membership agreement with the IUS was worked out in 1952 at the time when NUS was instrumental along with other Western European Unions in setting up the International Student Conference. Membership was finally terminated in 1955.

Long debates about NUS's international commitment, a growing anti-communism from the platform and a weakening of the Union characterised the ten years to 1955. It is difficult to recreate these circumstances. Cold war terminology discreetly purveyed in the minutes, innuendo, the incessant use of the word "partisan" and a determination that the NUS should not be "political", acted as a cover for the cold war offensive in the student world. 1945–55 were years when the NUS lost influence and support in the student body.

Specifically between 1949 and 1953 NUS declined by 20 per cent in its corporate membership. In 1946 there were 50,000 students affiliated; in 1949 some 105,000. In the period 1953–5 there were 80,000. Part of the reason for this decline was the attention given to international affairs at the expense of issues of more direct and immediate concern to the membership. Some large student unions left because of the withdrawal from the IUS, others because the withdrawal did not take place fast enough. Subsidiary factors may well have been the attitude of complete disinterest in the NUS taken by Florence Horsbrugh, Minister of Education, and the loss of the post-war generation of ex-servicemen from the student body—thereby depleting the calibre of student leadership. Undoubtedly, the main reason was the cold war. In 1952 the NUS leadership could only "record and regret" an adverse government decision on student grants and resolve that "the student body should share in the sacrifices which the community is called upon to make at the present time". The Student Labour Federation at the time commented that the membership could hardly be blamed for apathy or impatience. Certainly they would not be very interested in this sort of policy. Second-hand, thinly veiled cold war policies seeking to justify rearmament, Korea, etc., were not designed to lead to membership involvement.

During the 1955–65 decade the NUS developed its capacity as an educational pressure group in the formal sense. An expertise at memorandum presentation was developed. The grants policy was refined. The high point of this was the decision of the Anderson Committee in 1960 to recommend the abolition of the parental means test (which the Tory Government did not accept). However, in the contemporary sense the NUS did not campaign. This, it was asserted, would destroy the influence of the NUS in the appropriate places. The left throughout this time argued for a more militant posture. It was not until the economic and political climate for higher education became harder in the late 1960's that the NUS began to be less polite.

At the end of the war the NUS produced a major document calling on the Government to expand rapidly the universities. This was one of the major educational initiatives of the Union's history. Another was the activity in the late 1950's surrounding the setting up of the Robbins Committee. The NUS participated in joint activity with a wide range of educational organisations. The evidence of the Union to the Committee in 1961 is one of the most important documents the Union has ever produced. It clearly stated a number of current tenets of policy for the first time and many were involved in its preparation. It called for a rapid expansion of higher education. It did not, however, take a clear position on the binary distinction in post-school education. It urged an increase in the number of universities and the development of the training colleges within the university ambit. It said that "the siting of new universities would seem to provide an ideal opportunity for integrating existing non-university colleges into a broader structure", but there was no mention of comprehensive institutions. This and a full critique of the binary system were to develop a few years later in the context of polytechnic development and the rapid expansion of higher education in the public sector.

There can be no doubt that the cold war severely damaged the NUS. It was not just about breaking up the anti-fascist alliance, making an enemy of an erstwhile ally and using every means of hostility short of all-out war against the Soviet Union and the emerging socialist states—important as these objectives were. It had a domestic purpose—to undermine the militancy and radicalism in popular movements, to attack democratic rights (hence Macarthyism), to encourage docility and conformism, to divide communist from non-communist and to weaken thereby the overall movement, in the interests of the ruling class. For nearly twenty years the NUS suffered from anti-communism and all that this entailed. It narrowed and stunted its growth. The Union could not and did not want to involve the mass membership in a democratic or campaigning manner. It could not fully develop a radical educational policy because to do so would have meant both mass action and political discussion. The "no politics" rule meant in reality no left-wing politics and a tame union. The crunch point of this for those who led the NUS in these years was the IUS. At all costs it had to be opposed, isolated and weakened. Fortunately, however, the CIA paymasters were not able to make such anti-democratic inroads here as they were in some countries; no doubt efforts were made. In particular in the USA the looser structure of the US National Student Association enabled the CIA to corrupt a generation of student leaders and "buy" the organisation's politics, especially its international commitments.

Despite positive developments in the Union in the period leading up to the mid-sixties, ultimately its commitment to the International

Student Conference and against the International Union of Students was to be the undoing of the right-wing leadership. Their victory at the 1966 Exeter Conference in reversing the decision taken in November 1965 not to seek affiliation to the ISC was a pyrrhic one indeed. The Union was being asked by the leadership to make a political commitment to the ISC when at the same time an apolitical constitution was to be maintained for the NUS at home. Suspicion and opposition grew. Following the CIA revelations in 1967 anti-communism could no longer deliver the votes as easily as before. During the early 1960's the student body had begun to change. Demands for increased educational opportunity and expansion induced students to think more widely than their own careers. The ever present threat of nuclear war made a sizeable number participate in the Campaign for Nuclear Disarmament. The 1962 Cuba crisis and the arrogance of the United States unwilling to allow Cuba national independence and tolerate what it itself had imposed on the Soviet Union for over fifteen years, dented cold war ideology. Students began to demand more of their Union than cheap travel and politics by proxy at international conferences.

# 4

## THE STUDENT MOVEMENT, 1966–74

Huge developments in the student world have taken place in the past decade. In common with other comparable capitalist states students in Britain have become more militant, more active; a new political phenomenon has emerged. "Student unrest", "student militancy" have become the norm. The apathy and quiescence already described have been dispelled.

Things began to change in 1966 when the established right-wing manner in which the NUS was being run came under increasing attack. Experience of a variety of individuals—socialists, communists and liberals—led to a greater unity being formally established in the Radical Student Alliance. The RSA sought to give a lead to actions of students on a variety of questions of educational and wider concern. (See appendix 2 for its manifesto.) Specifically it sought to challenge the leadership of the NUS, which was opposed to campaigning in a mass way, to direct action, to a wider consideration of issues in a political context, and to radical reforms in the NUS structure and electoral system.

After October 1966, when the Alliance was formally created, two direct problems came up. The first was the escalating conflict at the London School of Economics—where students' rights of assembly and democratic self-government were increasingly baulked by the reactionary School authorities, and the Labour Government's draconian and thoroughly discriminatory policy of increasing fees charged to overseas students studying in Britain. The LSE dispute in its early stages demonstrated very clearly the new tactics and style to be deployed in the student movement. The first sit-in in Britain took place in March 1967 because the School would not permit a student union meeting to discuss the situation over the appointment of a new Director for LSE (Sir Walter Adams) on School premises. The interrelation between this democratic question, the political background of the individual as former Principal of University College Rhodesia and the character of the School's own government were a powerful stimulus to mass action. Only the RSA was prepared to undertake the necessary task of mobilising support for the LSE students.

The NUS leadership was even more compromised over the question of overseas students fees. Here the decision unilaterally (without consultation with other governments and educational agencies) to increase by up to 270 per cent what overseas students were charged aroused great hostility from students. It was a narrow chauvinistic and petty decision of Mr. Crosland's that many students saw as implicitly racialist. It was clearly shown that students were prepared to act in a national and mass way for the first time. Two major mobilisations (February 1st and 22nd, 1967) took place. Again the NUS leadership sought to "tone down" the action—"Leave it all to us, lads" was the appeal. Only the RSA and a number of local student union officers gave a lead.

Press reaction to these early developments was predictably hostile. After a peaceful and orderly demonstration the *Daily Express* (2/2/67) said that the "disorderly" students should be "cleared out". *The Times* pontificated that "a student is a student", i.e. students had no business to do anything else but study. Students taking action for the first time were both surprised and angered by this. *The Times'* response to legitimate policies was insulting and added fuel to the fire of radicalism. The novelty of student unrest and the exaggerated publicity served to strengthen the movement. For the moment at least it could be excused the luxury of basking in the free space granted by somewhat incredulous journalists. The almost obsessive concern for "respectability" by the NUS leadership provided an excellent foil.

The RSA was an *ad hoc* organisation—a loose coalition of liberal, socialist, communist and student union elements. It had little formal structure, merely a national council to co-ordinate and an annual convention to which all supporters were invited. This suited the student milieu and the organisation of mass action at the time. Yet, despite attempts to give it greater organisational resource, it was wound up in 1969 (though its constituent parts continued as an "NUS Commission" which ultimately in 1973 formed into the "Broad Left").

Another weakness and paradoxical strength lay in the Radical Alliance's policy and theory. Apart from seeking to put teeth into NUS policies and widen their political context its main contribution was the notion of student power. This was a somewhat vague importation from the USA. Its weakness was that it led some to believe that students should above all else control the colleges and universities. Yet its strident assertion of student rights was apposite to the developing mass movement. Students should no longer be subject to paternalistic college regimes (*in loco parentis*), archaic regulations and the like. They wanted to be able to control their own lives. After its mobilising role in the 1967 Spring term, RSA served little more than as a focal point for the battles taking place within the NUS framework. Its achievement was dual. It catalysed the early crucial developments of the mass movement, and it set in motion the changes in the NUS to bear fruit two years later.

A contributory reason for the weakening of the RSA was the setting up of a rival organisation, the Revolutionary Socialist Student Federation, in June 1968. Some who had supported the RSA thought it should have adopted a more explicitly socialist orientation and objected to its concern to secure changes in the NUS and student unions. The manifestations and novelty of mass action, combined with idle and provocative media talk of "student revolution", led to a feeling amongst some on the left that students could lead the proverbial "storming of the gates of heaven".

The manifesto of the organisation (set out in appendix 3) clearly reveals a view that students are a vanguard of revolution. Whilst these views are dealt with in greater depth in the next chapter it is important to note that the RSSF *wrote off* student unions and trade unions. It called for the setting up of "new participatory mass-based organisations" to lead the struggle. Their approach was largely a university-oriented one, accepting, as the media did at the time, that students were synonymous with university students.

It is important to recall that the RSSF secured the majority of its support from so called Trotskyist and Maoist organisations and their supporters. Having dismissed student unions and the NUS as irrelevant or "counter revolutionary" organisations they changed their view two years later, becoming involved with them as their leaderships, orientation and activities changed. The International Socialism group, one of the main supporters of the RSSF (in *Education, Capitalism and the Student Revolt*, 1969) had asserted: "The official Union, the NUS, can play no role here." But in 1972 they argued in their pamphlet *Students and the Struggle for Socialism* that "its existence is vital to the counter-offensive of the militant students". It is my view that this organisation and others like it adopt a fundamentally opportunist position towards both student unions and the NUS. They would quite willingly connive with their splitting on "political" lines. As the IS say, setting out their revolutionary scenario: "In those circumstances it would be absurd to imagine that the NUS could accommodate revolutionaries and counter-revolutionaries. There would undoubtedly be a split" (*Students and the Struggle for Socialism*). The views and actions of the "revolutionaries" as opposed to the "counter-revolutionaries" are placed above the needs of the mass movement.

The overriding impression gained of the RSSF was that what "revolutionaries" thought and said was of paramount importance. Seemingly it was enough for the "revolutionaries" to want something to happen for it to happen. Intensity of a belief was sufficient substitute for either an objective assessment of a given situation or a strategy for dealing with it. Hand in hand with this approach was the notion of "propaganda of the deed". As Paul Hoch, in *The Natives are Restless*, argued: "We believe *the revolution is ourselves*; it is not just getting the message to the moderates, or winning the left liberals, but furthering our own development, every step of the way, from student activists to the real thing. Unlike the official preachers of revolution we believe revolutionaries are developed by more and more militant *actions* not just by adopting official rhetoric or joining brand new revolutionary sects" (Hoch's emphasis). The duty of revolutionaries "was to make revolution", apparently without the participation of the mass of people, let alone students.

In the end the whole house of cards collapsed in ignominious sectarian strife. Big words and adventurist acts were not enough. The RSSF taught the student movement how things ought *not* to be done.

In 1968 there was a unique concatenation of events—the continued US barbarity in Vietnam and the heroic Tet offensive of the National Liberation Front, the increasingly disastrous record of the Wilson Labour Government, the example of Che Guavara and the apparent example of the role of youth and students in political action in China, France, Czechoslovakia and elsewhere. Domestic problems facing students in Britain began to become more acute. In a variety of struggles, particularly at the Hornsey and Guildford Schools of Art, the bases of important reforms were laid. Historically both positive and negative aspects coexisted uneasily. One cannot underestimate the role of the media here. They did two things. They spread information about what was going on. At the same time they determined the substance of much that students did. Their talk of "student revolution" made students' activities assume "revolutionary" proportions in their own minds. The cultural cult of youth only made the illusion stronger. Jerry Rubin in *Do It* expressed how some students saw things: "Every revolutionary needs a colour TV: Walter Cronkite is SDS's best organiser. Uncle Walter brings out the map of US with circles around campuses which blew up today. Every kid out there is thinking, 'Now I wanna see *my* campus on that map'. Television proves the domino theory—one campus falls and they all fall." Unfortunately Walter Cronkite was not a revolutionary and he served other interests.

What happened in France was particularly influential in Britain. Gross overcrowding, antiquated syllabuses and a totally inadequate system of student support had for years made for pent-up anger and frustration among the French students. The maturing crisis of Gaullism and the build-up of industrial action, culminating in the CGT demonstration of May 1st, 1968, led to the massive and spectacular student unrest in *les événements* of May–June. Excessive police brutality, the popular outrage and massive trade union action led to important gains being won.

Similar events took place in other countries, notably Italy, Western Germany and the USA. In Italy the most violent unrest took place in Turin, Milan and Rome. The physical conditions and backwardness of higher educational institutions in Italy probably exceeds even the French. In the early months of 1968 student manifestations in West Germany reached a peak in violent confrontations with the police, attacks on the premises of the Springer press, notorious for its bigoted and extremely hostile coverage of students, and ultimately the shooting of one of the student leaders, Rudi Dutschke. Student unrest in the United States covered perhaps the widest range of issues, reached its greatest intensity over the aggression in Vietnam, and assumed its most bizarre social and cultural proportions (as opposed to political)—drugs, flower power, etc.

What general conclusions can be drawn from this international experience?:

1. National representative student organisations in comparable

capitalist countries were weaker than in Britain. Student unionism has stronger historical roots here. In Italy no student unions of any substantial sort existed in 1968. In the US the CIA had subverted the National Student Association, UNEF in France was a minority movement, while VDS in Western Germany had been even more compromised by right-wing leadership than the NUS. Only in Western Germany did the National Union have any stable source of finance. One of the prime targets of student activity were the established student organisations. This attack was more effective than could have been the case here, though at Hornsey and Guildford one of the first acts of the students was to destroy their (albeit very inadequate) unions. They then spent another year laboriously reconstructing them.

2. Student unrest abroad was more intense, more violent and more political in content. Violent repression from state agencies did not occur to the same degree in Britain. A larger minority of students in other countries were committed to radical/revolutionary change, though the acid test of history reveals that they were not particularly effective in achieving much either in a broad political or specific educational direction. Tactics of minority mobilisations, confrontationism and an inability to forge links with the working-class movement contributed to this.

3. These "explosions" were relatively ephemeral, the most violent and apparently committed actions were soon followed by quiescence. These student movements were volatile, tended to concentrate on specific issues or disputes and lacked organisational resources. The dominant organisational forms employed were *ad hoc* or even spontaneous—the politics of non-organisation. In Italy a loose *Movimento Studentesco* was the centre piece of the actions. In Western Germany there was a loose federation of socialist, anarchist and communist elements—the SDS occupied the leadership. In the USA Students for a Democratic Society, more radical-liberal than Marxist, had a loose and decentralised structure. In France the National Union, UNEF, competed with a host of sectarian grouplets for the leadership, the mass of students owing it no particular allegiance. Loose organisations are fine for particular campaigns but they cannot sustain a mass movement for any period of time. Ad-hocery may appeal to

those who fear bureaucracy more than anything else and enjoy or are capable of only the politics of sectariana. But all the above-mentioned organisations, like the RSSF, dissolved in sectarian disarray and the mass of students was left without leadership or democratic organisation and with a pessimistic assessment of the possibilities of the student movement.

Both in this country and abroad student unrest since the late 1960's has focused around local issues and disputes. Their central importance is demonstrated by the fact that it is in the colleges and universities that students' actions can have their most direct effect. Four types of issue have been important:

(a) Matters relating to facilities and finance: in the last two or three years actions over facilities, grants and hall fees have assumed a greater importance than previously on account of the worsening position of educational expenditure. Formerly these matters were thought by many on the left to be unimportant in comparison with more political and ideological issues. Now rent strikes, catering boycotts and inadequate accommodation are basic to the struggle of the student movement. Indeed it is usually the case that matters of autonomy of student organisation and victimisation of student leaders are interwoven with essentially financial questions—disputes broadening out from this starting point, e.g. Essex University, 1973–4; Keele, 1972–3.

(b) Student Union Autonomy: throughout the recent period the right of students to decide who their leaders are and what they should say has been central. These issues more than anything else—and the fight against authorities who desire to curtail autonomy—have caused the greatest number of local disputes. In 1966 David Adelstein, President of the Students Union of LSE, was disciplined for carrying out the wishes of those he represented in writing to *The Times* and stating the views of the Union. In 1972 Linda Quinn, President of the Stirling University Students' Association, was disciplined because she had failed "to keep due order" at a meeting which had decided on action appropriate to the Queen's visit to Stirling. At Nonington College of Physical Education in the same year a protracted conflict took place over whether the union could have a president who was sabbatical or not. As in the trade union world, victimisation of elected representatives is intolerable.

(c) More explicitly political questions, e.g., the Vietnam war, racialism, have been less important than the foregoing. They have constituted a general backcloth. Perhaps the most political question animating local disputes in Britain was the question of secret files in 1970. At the University of Warwick it was discovered that the authorities had been keeping political files on students and staff. Concern spread throughout the student body. This in a far wider context threw into question the right of any authority or employer to store confidential information about individuals.

(d) Educational issues—student representation, assessment and academic freedom—are the last area. There have been relatively few local conflicts where educational issues of curriculum and assessment in the narrow sense have generated disputes. Hornsey and Guildford Colleges of Art in 1968, and subsidiary to them a number of other art establishments, showed that art students had an intense concern for the content of their education, which they subjected to a thoroughgoing criticism.

This more than anything else was the positive achievement of student unrest in the summer of 1968. In the Spring term of both 1972 and 1973 students in the Economics Faculty of Cambridge University took direct action over the reform of assessment procedures. The university obstinately resisted any move away from traditional time-test examinations. Of greater importance perhaps has been the general question of academic freedom and the restrictions placed on left-wing lecturers—specifically the sacking of Robin Blackburn at the LSE, of Dick Atkinson at Birmingham University and (attempted) of David Craig at Lancaster University. Despite protestations to the contrary from right-wing sources, it is against left and radical lecturers that the authorities have attempted to clamp down. Students have been in the vanguard in defending academic freedom and supporting lecturers who are both popular and good teachers.

Most important of all, then, has been the general theme of democratisation of the institutions of higher and further education, with quite legitimate demands for unfettered student self-government and student representation on broader educational and political matters. Usually a specific series of factors combine to give a powerful impact—crass behaviour by a college authority, a political implication and perceived student rights. It is this combination that gives the legitimacy and power to student action.

The end of the previous chapter made clear that the NUS and student unions were beginning to need radical reform. In the mid 1960's there were a number of areas of dispute between the leadership and the left wing as exemplified by the RSA. The right-wing leadership's conception of the role of NUS was that the Union should act as an informed educational pressure group with minimal active involvement of the membership. Its philosophy was "students as such"; students were seen in isolation from other sections of society and, particularly, they were to have no connection with politics, at least not through their union organisations. Politics was for party political organisations. This led the right wing to fight against any campaign proposed which sought to broaden involvement of the membership in any active way.

There were three or four long standing areas of conflict—the Union's voting system for Executive elections, the NUS's international commitments and the Union's constitutional aims and objects. All reflected a wider crisis of confidence in the leadership and the type of union they wished to preserve. For fifteen years the NUS Executive had sustained itself in power by a peculiarly undemocratic voting method (multiple transferable voting) which ensured that a majority of the Conference could elect all the members of the Executive. The alternative championed by the left wing was single transferable voting, whereby the leadership would become more representative of the membership as a whole. After several nearly successful attempts the change took place in 1969.

The leadership's commitment to the International Student Conference was mentioned in chapter 3. Their position of "students as such" for the membership at home and a free hand abroad for an openly anti-communist policy for themselves became increasingly contradictory. Pointed questions about the dubious American funds from which the ISC secured much of its money and the subsequent revelations of the leaders of the United States National Student Association in February 1967, exposed the ISC as a fraud and a front for international CIA subversion. The ISC folded up in 1969.

Many attempts had been made to alter the NUS's clause 3. For some time the Union had been weakened by its inability to frame policies and action in anything but the narrowest context. Presenting grants claims and being told by governments that they could not be afforded because other non-educational items of expenditure were more important, made for both political and strategic weakness. The Government was not constrained by "students as such" considerations; why should the NUS be? More importantly the questions of moral and political concern, e.g., racialism, caused it not to attract the interest of increasing numbers of progressive and activist students. NUS's aims and objects were broadened in 1969.

In 1967–8 events were passing the NUS by. Increasingly developments of significance were taking place outside the NUS and student union contexts. Old style debating and representative council student politics became increasingly inappropriate. At a political level the NUS leadership opposed the major manifestations of the student movement and restricted structural changes which would allow for a greater democratic responsiveness in the NUS structure. In 1968–9 student unions began to reform their mode of government to allow for greater use of general meetings, as opposed to SRC's. They sought to change their constitutions and become more like trade unions for students, and less like imitation parliamentary debating shops. The entrenched right-wing "socialite" leaderships began to be removed.

For the NUS leadership the writing was on the wall. A number of specific events lead to their downfall in 1969–70. Geoff Martin's (President 1966–8) "abrasive" and provocative style of leadership lost credibility; the vacillating and undecisive 1968 grants campaign, where the membership, probably willing to respond, was given no lead; the reaction to the Summer 1968 events of seeking agreements with college authorities, rather than focusing discontent; the sell out of the embattled Hornsey and Guildford students; the unconstitutional condemnation of the massive October 27th, 1968, Vietnam demonstration by Martin and the unwillingness to assist LSE students in 1969 Spring term. The old guard began to break up. Left manœuvres by the aspirant presidential candidate Fisk only made things worse. They were no longer able to carry on in the old way. The electorate in April 1969 deduced this and voted for Jack Straw. Soon afterwards there was a majority left leadership.

Since that time the NUS has occupied the centre of the stage of student politics. Increasingly it has assumed the roles of forum, leader and organiser for the student movement. It has begun to fulfil its potential and utilise its financial and organisational resources in the full service of the mass movement. For the first time in relation to disputes at University College Swansea and the University of Manchester in February 1970, the NUS gave unequivocal support to local unions in dispute. More especially in the aftermath of Hornsey and Guildford in 1969, Lancaster University in 1972 and Stirling in 1973, NUS intervention assumed an organisational and mass form. It did far more than give political support and sympathy. The newly established legal aid fund became an important weapon in defending individuals from attacks from college authorities.

In the period 1966–9 the student movement was largely localised, college-based and issue-orientated. With the changes that had taken place in the Union it now became possible for the movement to develop a more pronounced national character. In 1972–3 major national campaigns based on large-scale mobilisations took place on student union autonomy and grants. In 1972 mass demonstrations and much other unrest took place which forced the Tory Government to shelve its plans for hamstringing the student unions. In 1973–4, on the grants question, a national rent strike, occupations and a national one-day student strike were promoted. These resulted in obtaining an interim grants increase in 1973 and major reforms to the grants system in 1974, particularly on the matter of discretionary awards.

The NUS's policies moved to the left at the same time. In 1970 a comprehensive policy on the trade union movement was adopted. The Union is a central point in the campaign against apartheid, for women's rights and on a number of other matters. Reviewing the period covered by this chapter it can be said that student unions and the NUS as the basic organisations of the student movement have responded and adapted to underlying social and economic trends in the student body. In retrospect 1966–8 laid the basis for subsequent advances and demonstrated a number of lessons still relevant today.

# 5

## THE CHARACTER OF THE STUDENT MOVEMENT

There can be no doubt that the student movement has grown in Britain over the last decade. It has become more active, politically significant and subject to much attack. Consideration of this has largely been at a superficial level, being concerned more with the form of actions than their content and underlying causes. This chapter attempts to look deeper. There can be no full evaluation except in a wide political canvas. A narrow sociological approach will not do. So it is necessary to look at developments in the context of the views and policies of the major political parties involved and to treat them in some measure polemically. This is how the issues exist in the student movement.

A variety of rather frivolous reasons for student unrest have been presented from time to time. Timothy Raison, MP, suggested that progressive primary school teaching methods and generational conflict were responsible. Edward Short thought that loneliness of students coming straight from school into adult institutions was important. Philip Toynbee thought the "eruptions" of 1968 were more religious than economic and political. The Monday Club has blamed it all on the communists. Dr. Spock's child-rearing methods have likewise been held responsible, the "permissive society" and so on. The substantial causes are, however, to be found within the system of higher education, the students' own circumstances, the experience of students and their organisations and the political developments that have taken place in British capitalism. There are, I think, ten interrelated reasons which are substantial.

1. The sheer increase in size of the colleges and universities, the institution of new colleges and new universities, new courses, etc., have had two results. First, established practices of administration, teaching and so on have not changed as fast as the students have demanded. Second, changes themselves have led students to question what is going on, because they themselves are a part of the change, because it affects them more directly than anybody else, and they should have a say in the

way the decisions are taken. Processes of change have also induced students to think more critically about the institutions around them. This is part of the origin of demands for representation and participation. These demands in themselves have, if refused and fought for, been powerful agencies of change.

2. The worsening material conditions of students have led them no longer to accept inadequate grants, housing, etc., simply because they are told to do so or because the privilege of a higher/further education makes it worth the suffering.

3. A potent factor changing students' attitudes towards their education is the altered circumstances students find themselves in when they leave college and university. No longer is the degree or certificate an "open sesame" to a good job, a high salary and a guaranteed career. It remains so for some but for many expectations have had to change. The status of being a student is not as secure as it was. For many entering a career such as teaching, the question is particularly sharp.

4. Over the last thirty years there has been a marked change in attitudes towards education; the educational attainment of young people today is far higher than it was thirty years ago. The expansion of educational opportunity and provision since the 1944 Education Act, and most importantly, the battles and campaigns around these changes (primary and nursery school provision, against the 11-plus, for comprehensive secondary education, etc.) have led many parents and young people to regard education as a right rather than a privilege. The students of the 1960's were the first generation to reach adulthood after the 1944 Act. In one sense student actions on educational issues are a historical continuation of the earlier battles on primary and secondary education. Viewing education as a right, it is much more likely that students will examine critically what they receive. They are less likely to take things as given. This educational change has gone hand in hand with a wider change amongst young people associated with earlier physical and emotional maturation. The Family Law Reform Act and the lowering of the age of majority have reinforced this. Most students are legally adults and expect to be treated as such, given the adult responsibilities they now bear.

5. The last decade has been one of titanic political struggles and conflicts, nationally and internationally. The overall situation has been one of constant change; the heroic struggle of the Vietnamese for national liberation, Cuba, detente, the worsening problems of poverty and overpopulation, apartheid, US imperialism, the Popular Unity Government in Chile, etc. In this country the rising tide of working-class militancy, racialism, the conflicts in Northern Ireland and other questions have all affected students, the more politically aware and leading sections in particular. The crisis which has been continuous at an economic and political level has had its effect on the thinking of all. To students the more moral aspects have been especially important, e.g., successive governments' Vietnam policies, racialism and Powellism, apartheid, etc.

6. In relation to 5, particularly during the early stages of development, the performance of right-wing social democracy in government and the NUS had a potent effect, not only in radicalising students, but also determining the direction in which they have moved. Some, naïvely perhaps, have rejected the Labour Party *in toto*. Others have rejected Parliament as a valid area of activity for the left. The hypocrisy and immorality of Labour politicians defending US imperialism in Vietnam, advocating increased trade with South Africa, bashing the unions and giving large handouts to big business, has revolted many student activists in the Labour Party. Contradictions like these made some more left-wing, others disillusioned.

7. The student body, particularly in the last three years, has been subject to attack. This has led student politics to be more practical, organised and powerful. Union autonomy, grants and other struggles over the rights and living conditions of students have identified the Government and the state as the enemy.

8. A powerful factor in the radicalisation of students has been a whole host of local developments—victimisations, fund freezing, refusals to implement desired reforms and so on. The behaviour of college authorities in not meeting student demands has been fundamentally important.

9. No one involved with students in recent years could fail to notice some of the profound cultural changes that have taken place. Students share these in common with other young people. Dress styles, music and dance are more assertive, energetic and expressive. On the one hand the social and political importance for the mass movement has been very great—they accompanied, were intertwined with it and gave it a wider identity and self expression. At the same time drugs, excessive individualism and libertarianism have been politically negative by-products. Sexuality, the rights and position of women and gay people are increasingly becoming political issues themselves.

10. Perhaps most important of all, the role and purpose of higher education has changed. The basic reason for the post-Robbins expansion was the need of employers and capitalism in general for a greater variety and number of highly skilled (and educated) manpower. This in turn has been dictated by the technical changes that have taken place in production resulting in increased automation, larger enterprises, monopoly control and the growth of service industries. The institutions of higher and further education are now of greater political concern to the state. They play an increasingly important economic role in preparing employees "suitably". Students are no longer the sons and daughters of the rich obtaining an education suiting them for a career of idleness or a position in the "liberal professions" (with a few bright students on scholarships from other sections of the population providing sufficient academics and teachers). Students now comprise over 20 per cent of the age-group. Students are not the élite they were. A degree does not buy what it used to. Circumstances of students are now more difficult. They have responded to a new situation, acted in defence of their own interests and become involved in much wider issues. Perhaps it is the uncertainty more than anything else which has radicalised the students. It cannot be emphasised strongly enough that these changes have been basically *mass* in character. For although different elements and sections of the student body have responded to pressures in different ways, it does not alter the fact that all have been affected.

### Students and the working class

Students are a definite social group. They are defined as a group by social attitudes and in objective terms. They are generally young. Most, but by no means all, are the sons and daughters of professional and administrative workers. They receive grants in various forms. They experience a range of common educational problems. They have an individual and a corporate status in the colleges and universities. As a social group they can play a very important political role. Lenin talked of students in pre-revolutionary Russia as an "indicator", a section of the population which by its activity indicated the level of general crisis in society. Under fascist dictatorship the heroism of students can be an example, as in Greece in 1972–3. Their ease of mobilisation (and sometimes demobilisation) makes it easier for students than some other sections of the population to undertake demonstrative activities.

In making an assessment of students in a wider social context it is important to consider three aspects: the social background of students, the social destination of students and students as students. It is naïve to say that "they're all middle class" because they come in the main from middle-class and middle-strata backgrounds. Similarly the view that they're all Tories because some may vote that way in future, or that they are somehow a *déclassé* intelligentsia "because students as students do not relate in any direct way to production", or that they are all "revolutionaries". In all three aspects the students' position is changing. As the means of production come more and more into monopoly hands, ever wider sections of the population are objectively forced into an anti-monopoly position in order to protect their interests. As the process of technological change develops, so the proportion of the labour force not engaged in manual labour increases and the number requiring specialist skills and training increases. Science and technology once merely incidental to capitalist production are now central to its maintenance and development. As monopoly employs increasing numbers of scientists, technologists and administrators it becomes more necessary for these individuals to become unionised. Their interests can no longer be served solely on the basis of their dealing with employers on an individual basis. White-collar and scientific, administrative and educational unions have grown, become more organised and their memberships more prepared to take industrial action. In this process of change established patterns of political and social behaviour are being modified.

Students are in the majority potential trade unionists. Teaching, the biggest single occupation that students enter, has been marked by an increase in unionisation in recent years. Students are not immune to the above changes themselves, though their specific application in the educational context is different. The strengthening of student unions can be seen to parallel the growth of white-collar unionism. Yet because of the fluidity of the students' position, the transitional and transitory nature of the student body, what students themselves do is important in marking out their class position. In Marxist terms a class position or role is not a static structural entity in isolation, it relates to the class struggle between those who own the means of production and those who do not. The class position of students is in some measure determined by how they as a mass relate to the working class or the ruling class. One of the results of the ten points enumerated above is that students as a mass incline more to the working-class movement than previously. The working class needs allies to wage the class struggle successfully. Likewise students have to find friends and support within and without higher education if their campaigns are to have a successful outcome. In addition to these objective factors a range of particular points must be added which strengthen the change, e.g., the political affiliation of individuals and groups, the exigencies of particular campaigns, particular issues of joint interest, e.g., industrial training and part-time further education, the health service, associate student membership of trade unions, etc.

"Are students workers?" is a question sometimes asked. But is this question one which will allow a meaningful answer to be given? Students are not workers, yet the character of the working class is itself changing. As monopoly capitalism develops wider sections of the population are drawn into the working class.

Are student unions trade unions? What of student trade unionism? Student unions are not trade unions in the narrow sense of the term. They are organisations which are increasingly seeking to defend and advance the interests of their members and undertaking other activities of a trade union type. Sections of the organised trade union movement would not have regarded themselves as trade unionists until recently, e.g., teachers, local government officers. Tenants' organisations, claimants' unions, women's organisations, pensioners' associations, etc., are not trade unions, but they are bodies that defend and advance the interests of their members, in the main working-class people. They form an indispensable part of the organised strength in the working class and labour movements.

"Can student unions intervene in the class struggle?" might be another question asked by those who are still unconvinced of the positive role of student unions. The answer is that they don't intervene, they're in it. Campaigns of solidarity with the labour movement, campaigns for student grants, demands for increased educational opportunity, all have an impact on the overall balance of class forces, nationally and internationally. It must be remembered that the class struggle pervades all aspects and levels of society, it is not something that is to be found only at the points of production and the extraction of surplus value. "Student trade unionism" was a term first coined in 1966 which, along with "student syndicalism" and "student power", was used to indicate the way in which radical and left elements wanted the student movement to progress. In particular, and quite rightly, the trade union movement was looked to as an example. Its solidarity and cohesion were seen as something desirable to develop in the student movement. It is clear now that all these original slogans had major weaknesses, although they fulfilled a valuable purpose at the time. The most expressive term in the present context is "student unionism", referring to the experience of student unions in defending and advancing the interests of their members.

A basis for unity between students and the working class exists as never before, and to some extent is has been realised. But it would be quite wrong to assume that there is no backlog of prejudice and difficulty still to be overcome. With the right policies and persistent, patient work these can begin to be tackled.

## The Communist Party of Great Britain

The Communist Party has played an active role in the student movement for many years. In recent years its membership in this area has grown considerably. In 1959 it had less than 200 student members, now there are over 1,000. It is the largest and best organised left-wing organisation amongst students. It has a record of policy on higher and further education, in particular its submission to the Robbins Committee and *Higher Education in the Nuclear Age*. It has argued for the democratisation of post-school education by widening access and making the government of the colleges and universities more democratic.

As a result of the cold war the Party's strength in the student movement was weakened. In the 1930's and 1940's it had occupied a leading position. During the 1950's the polarisation of the cold war forced the Party to concern itself with a limited number of issues in the NUS context—defending the Soviet Union and socialist countries, fighting against the isolation of the International Union of Students. It was only at the beginning of the 1960's that the situation began to change and the Party to overcome its relatively isolated position. It played a crucial role in the formation of the Radical Student Alliance. After protracted discussion it decided against involvement in the Revolutionary Socialist Students Federation, and it is now an important element in the Broad Left coalition of students.

The Communist Party considers that the mass of students is capable of mobilisation on a consistent basis in defence of student interests, and likewise of seeing these interests in a wider context—in relation to the labour movement, educational reform, democratic questions and international issues. The emphasis is particularly laid on the mass aspect, for student conditions and aspirations will not be protected or advanced by pressure-group activities in isolation. The relationship to the working-class movement is not to be one of "detonator", or of "vanguard". Students cannot constitute themselves the leadership of the working-class movement, nor is their relationship with it of a political nature only. But it is objectively in the interests of the mass of students to seek an alliance with the working class. It is only with the support of the trade union movement that student demands can be adequately satisfied.

The Communist Party's programme, *The British Road to Socialism*, argues that the working class needs to form a wide popular alliance in the struggle for socialism. "It is necessary and possible to build a broad popular alliance around the leadership of the working class, fighting every aspect of the policies of the monopolies; to develop a wide movement for peace, democracy and improvement in living standards, and for a democratic programme which leads in the direction of socialism . . . such an alliance is an essential condition for the establishment of a real socialist government to build a Socialist Britain."

The Communist Party has understood the relationship of students with the working-class movement in this light. Given the mass character of the student issues, it is best for the relationship with the working class to take organised forms. In particular this means the development of a multiplicity of links, national and local, between student unions and trade unions. The range of common interests between students and trade unionists and their organisations is increasing. Organised contacts have the advantage of being durable, reciprocal and most suited to the task of overcoming prejudices about students that exist in sections of the working class, and about trade unions amongst some students. Of course, the Party does not see the relationship solely in terms of establishing trade union–student union links. The expansion of the Party's own membership is crucial. So are particular campaigns of solidarity, e.g., with the miners in 1972 and 1974; wider political issues such as Vietnam and the Common Market; and contacts between individual students and trade unionists.

Ultimately, an NUS association with the TUC will be a major factor taking the unity much further forward. Even this in itself is not the only objective. Every possible means of extending contact should be employed. And false antagonisms must be avoided—such as that posed by the International Socialists who are in favour of working class-student unity but against the NUS affiliating to the TUC.

As long ago as 1945 the Communist Party appreciated the potentialities of the student unions and the NUS. "Communist students have a deep appreciation of the democratic nature of student unions, NUS and the Scottish NUS," wrote Peter Heaf, Chairman of the Communist Party National Student Committee, in the Spring 1945 issue of *Student Forward*. "They work to extend these democratic organisations to the students of those Technical, Art, Training and Domestic Science Colleges in which the students have as yet little or no opportunities for self-expression and self-government."

Student unions provide a democratic framework and resources which are indispensable for the successful prosecution of any campaign. At a national level the essential leadership, co-ordination and unity can be and have been supplied through the framework and actions of the NUS. The Party has sought to strengthen the left trend in the student unions and to make them more democratic and autonomous, in particular by the extension of the use of general meetings.

So in 1965 Fergus Nicholson, then Communist Party student organiser, wrote in a report to the Party's executive committee that the student unions were "the bodies through which students conduct their struggles and take action to obtain higher grants, abolition of the means test, greater democratic rights, etc., and contribute to national efforts for better education. . . . Communists have played an active part in many of the more militant unions." And in 1973 Dave Cook wrote in the pamphlet *Students*: "If we look at the places where large-scale mass action has taken place, such as Leicester and Birmingham in 1968, Manchester and Warwick in 1970, at Lancaster and Brighton in 1972, and Stirling in 1973, the student union has been the crucial debating chamber where the issue has been thrashed out and around which the action has been organised."

The Party has worked for left unity between socialists, militants, radicals and communists in the student movement (though it does not go beyond limited tactical agreements from time to time with Trotskyist and Maoist groups who, while avowedly socialist, have a conception of unity which precludes everyone except themselves and those very close to them, believing that anything not ultra-left "dilutes the programme" and would render unity "unprincipled"). Left unity is an objective which has to be attained if the short-term campaigns are to be fully successful. It is also a principle which must apply if advances towards socialism are to take place. As a revolutionary party seeking to overthrow capitalism by class struggle, the Communist Party sees itself as having a crucial role, yet at the same time as ineffective in isolation. Unity of the working class, unity of a wider popular alliance, unity on the left are all essential prerequisites.

So in the student union and NUS context the Party has played an active role in establishing and strengthening the "Broad Left", its journal, its conferences and other activities.

With all this there goes the Party's involvement in the ideological sphere. In the student unions and socialist societies it fights for the position and policies of practical and scientific communism. And communists seek to pose the socialist alternatives to the prevailing capitalist norms and axioms of the education which students receive. This activity takes many forms—meetings to draw up critiques of particular courses, the annual Communist University in London, theoretical articles in the journals, and so on.

In general, the Communist Party's strategy and activities over the past ten years have yielded successful results. In these years the student unions have been transformed, they have resisted the attacks of the Tory Government, and mass movements of a scale, militancy and political consciousness not known before have developed.

## The Labour Party

The Labour Party's record in student affairs is chequered. At no time in recent years has there been a Labour Party student organisation which reflected the strength of socialist and social democratic views amongst students. Prior to the proscriptions of the 1940's there existed a Student Labour Federation which was broadly based, produced journals, had full-time staff and engaged in a variety of campaigning activities (being very active at NUS Congresses). This was proscribed in 1947 by the Labour leadership, and another organisation— the National Association of Labour Student Organisations (NALSO)—was set up. In the latter 1950's and early 1960's this organisation began moving to the left due to the influence of the Campaign for Nuclear Disarmament and the declining influence of the cold war. NALSO became involved in mass-based activities and was associated with the formation of the RSA in 1966. In 1967 Transport House wound it up, partly because it had become too active for their liking and partly because of the sectarian antics of the Socialist Labour League who were trying to take it over. The SLL had already taken over the Young Socialists in 1964 resulting in its proscription. The sectarianism of the SLL played into the hands of Transport House and drove away many activists in disgust or boredom.

SALSO, the Scottish Federation of Labour Clubs, continued for some time and acted as a nucleus for future developments. An attempt was made in 1968 to form a National Federation of Socialist Societies. This was short lived. In 1969 the Labour Party's National Executive established a working party to investigate and report on the need for a national Labour Party student organisation. For two years socialist societies and Labour clubs existed, largely in isolation, and merging and splitting on a local basis. Some became associated with the RSSF. Meantime Labour Party Regional Youth Officers dispensed literature and assisted some of the Labour clubs. Then, with Transport House agreement, Students for a Labour Victory was formed by the individuals who composed the NEC working party. Its sole purpose was to generate student support for the Labour Party in the 1970

General Election. It made a number of statements that were critical of the 1964–70 Government.

In 1971 the National Organisation of Labour Students (NOLS) was formed. It was established as an organisation independent from the Labour Party, but at the same time it was to have a closer relationship with the Party and a higher status than had been previously held by NALSO. It was constituted with five objectives—"To secure support for the Labour Party in the various higher educational institutions; to advise the Labour Party National Executive Committee on Labour student organisation, educational matters and student opinion on matters of concern to the Labour Party; to assist in the formation and development of student Labour clubs and to encourage their liaison with the Labour Party Young Socialists and Constituency Labour Parties; to co-operate with the Labour Party Young Socialists in winning young people to socialism and the Labour Party; to propagate socialist views and the cause of the Labour Party in national organisations and elsewhere." The penultimate one is particularly important in the light of later developments. The report to the inaugural Conference added, "we must establish ourselves as a distinctive group in NUS aiming to guide its membership and organisation towards the Labour Movement and towards socialism. The NUT has joined the TUC and the NUS is moving in this direction. We must accelerate this process."

For a while NOLS gained in strength. It developed good relations with the NUS and took part in a number of campaigns, e.g., over grants and student union autonomy. But it gradually came under the influence of the so-called Militant Group. This was (and is) a Trotskyist group practising the strategy of "entrism"—that is, penetrating major working-class organisations with the objective of either taking them over or discrediting them. It has been particularly concerned with the Labour Party Young Socialists, which it effectively controls. Initially, there were three main political elements in NOLS—a group of right-wing careerists, a Tribune element and the Militant. The careerists were chiefly concerned each with his own future, and were not cohesive. The Tribunites were relatively unorganised and inexperienced. So there was a good opportunity for the Militant to get control—which they did. Campaigns became terribly "pure", and effectively there was no serious campaign against the Tories. In January 1974 the NOLS conference decided against any involvement in the Broad Left. And it looks as though, if this situation continues, NOLS will effectively opt out of the mass movement and become solely concerned with internal Labour Party conflicts—and risk being wound up. This no doubt suits the Labour Party right wing. Their total commitment to electoral politics, middle-of-the-road posture, non-militancy and non-mass involvement are bolstered by the antics of the Militant. Meantime the student movement suffers. For the right wing's inactivity and the *de facto* inactivity of Militant sectarianism are mutually reinforcing. Underneath all this is the problem that the Labour Party finds it difficult, in the absence of a coherent theoretical and ideological position, to attract young people—except the careerists and the species of Trotskyist that wants to try to take it over.

Yet this situation does not go unchallenged. A minority in NOLS oppose the Militant and are fully in favour of participation in the Broad Left and in a mass Labour Party student organisation. The situation is very fluid, and the Youth Committee of the Labour Party Executive has decided to mount a full-scale enquiry into the affairs of NOLS.

One aspect of the Labour Party's attitudes in student affairs should not go unmentioned. NUS leadership positions used to be an important route into Transport House and other right-wing niches in the Labour movement, and the Labour right wing regarded the NUS as a good training ground for ambitious young men. In view of this it is often hard to know whether the Labour leadership has any political perspective at all for the student movement. But a mass socialist student organisation with connections with the Labour Party would be an enormous asset in future struggles and in the overall perspective of achieving socialism.

In the Broad Left alliance of students the Labour Party left and the Communist Party are the two major organised elements. Together with these there are a number of non-aligned socialists who make a major contribution. The Broad Left is comparable with similar groupings existing in trade unions and other mass organisations. It represents an important area of agreement over principles and strategy. It seeks to draw the student movement closer to the organised working class; to back up and strengthen real militancy in the student world; to support and extend the democratisation of the NUS and the student unions; and to lead the mass movement to the left.

*The vanguard*

The view that students or youth in general form the revolutionary "vanguard" has had various support. It means that students/youth are either the revolutionary class, *or* the vanguard of that class, *or* a substitute for the role of the revolutionary party. In practice the distinction between these three separate notions is difficult to draw. In my experience only *The Times* has called students "a class", and then merely in a notional and unanalytical sense. The view that youth as a whole constitutes a class has been more commonly expressed in the United States than in Britain. At one time it was strongly espoused by the SDS. John and Margaret Rowntree (*International Socialist Journal*, February 1968) attempt to sustain the youth-class argument. Its basis seems to be that the young are more radical than the old and that they are more exploited than their elders—because of the importance of the "defence and education industries" within which youth clearly predominates. Their position was to a degree confused by their subsequent reference to youth as a "strategic sector". The youth-class idea can be seen as an extension of the more commonly held view that youth culture is a primary aspect of the lives of young people—at least more important than class, family and nationality ties.

The major purveyors of the idea of youth as a class or as a vanguard are the media. The press, commercial advertising and television unscrupulously idolise youth, make youth styles the paradigm by which all others are judged and set fashions, trends, etc., with youth primarily in mind. The youth market is big business. And there can be no denying the impact of the media on youth.

In the US the pressures are even more intense than in Britain. They were partly responsible for a section of the student body seriously believing that all over 30 could not be trusted and were enemies of the student movement. These points aside, youth in general has played a very important role in all the major conflicts of the twentieth century. Their contribution to the Russian revolution, to the Labour movement, to the anti-fascist struggles and to the cause of national liberation generally, has been of major significance.

The vanguard thesis has had three main advocates: *Black Dwarf* magazine and its supporters in 1968, Ernest Mandel and Herbert Marcuse.

Unlike Professors Mandel and Marcuse, *Black Dwarf* did not completely write off the leading role of the working class. But like them it saw a new phenomenon in the youth, particularly the student youth, and assumed that it had a revolutionary potential. Students were exhorted to "get on with it". In the editorial of June 13th, 1968, there was a call to arms: "Realism and imagination go hand in hand. The liberated university, the defeat of imperialism and the smashing of capitalism will follow." Indeed, Tom Nairn, who was close to *Black Dwarf*, and Angelo Quattrocchi developed the youth-vanguard thesis at some length in their *The Beginning of the End—France, May 1968*. "The production of consciousness," they announced, had replaced material production as the area of primary conflict in a class-divided society. The universities were seen as "the higher nervous system" of society. And they continued: "Marxism has remained aloof from the intellectual harbingers of the real revolution, in comfortable contemplation of the past ... although it is a general social contradiction certain ultimately to embrace the whole social body, it is natural that it should be focussed in higher education and initially spread in shock waves from the centre, awakening every latent contradiction of society.... These are the social conditions under which 'youth' can for the first time assume other than a biological meaning, a positive social meaning as the bearer of those pressures in the social body which prefigure a new society instead of the reproduction of the old one."

Professor Mandel, like all the Trotskyists, thought Paris in May 1968 was the socialist revolution in France, sold out by the French Communist Party. He argues that students are more likely than workers to develop a revolutionary consciousness. Part of the reason for this is that "the workers' movement does not erect multiple barriers against the penetration of bourgeois ideas ... most of the workers succumb, at least in normal conditions". Mandel continues (*Black Dwarf*, May 31st, 1968): "However, in amongst students, a larger minority, *precisely because they are in a more privileged social and intellectual position than the workers*, can free themselves by individual thought from the constant manipulation and mental conditioning of the general public opinion moulding instruments in the service of bourgeois society and capitalism. ... They can and they must play a powerful role as detonator. By playing this role within the working class, above all through the intermediary of the young workers, *they can free* in the working class itself enormous forces for challenging capitalist society and the bourgeois state." Whilst Mandel can be excused getting a little carried away in front of the students (his lecture was delivered in May in the Latin Quarter of Paris—see also his pamphlet *The Changing Role of the Bourgeois University*) he has regurgitated the classic petty bourgeois view that only the petty bourgeois are able to really understand what is going on, that theirs rather than the workers' is the realm of ideas—a "you provide the muscle and we'll provide the brains" approach.

It is to Herbert Marcuse, however, that the view of students as a revolutionary vanguard is most commonly attributed. Marcuse, not unlike Mandel, considers that the working class of capitalist countries has become completely absorbed into the system. Its revolutionary potential has been nullified permanently or temporarily (on this point he is contradictory). Instead, the revolutionary vanguard is to be the underprivileged peasants of the third world, disaffected minorities and the radical middle-class intelligentsia or students. These three diverse groups have reason to want the total destruction of the system. The working class has been bought off with material goods, brainwashed and integrated into the system to the point of supporting it.

There are, indeed, many variants of the theory that students are the vanguard of the revolution, the detonator, the catalyst, the brains, the conscience, etc. On the one hand there is the view that students can teach or lead workers to the revolution. On the other there is the view that it is the intensity of student action which sparks or provokes a crisis which in turn causes the workers to rise. These ideas are leftist or anarchistic in essence. They relegate the role of the working class to the back seat. They place a premium on the daring act and perpetual commitment and largely disregard the objective situation of class conflict. Still more they denigrate organisation. They are based on experiences and attitudes which are best described as petty bourgeois or middle class. Many supporters of these views are themselves new to political struggle and get carried away in enthusiasm over the revolutionary potential the struggle seems to contain—only to be deflated later on when this is not realised. These ideas can be harmless. They can also be extremely dangerous, confuse and divide the working-class and the student movement, and play into the hands of reaction.

*Red bases*

Some mention has been made of the idea of "Red Bases" in chapter 3. This was the major theoretical and strategic innovation of the Revolutionary Socialist Students Federation. Some have held that red bases actually existed in 1968–9, others have disagreed. But few ever put pen to paper on the theme, and the historical record is limited to three articles in the *New Left Review* of January–February 1969.

David Triesman defined the red base as follows: "In the first place, the red base is both inward looking and outward looking. It is the former because it becomes a secure zone within a hostile society for the length of the time it can be held. It allows an area to be consecrated in the name of revolution in which the formulation of an entire alternative ideology, carried on the back of essential demands, can be instigated."

David Fernbach saw it in terms of students making the link with the working class at the "revolutionary political level," as a consequence of which (i) bourgeois liberalism can be replaced by Marxism as the dominant ideology among the student mass; and (ii) real power can be won via mass mobilisation over courses and exams, over college buildings and facilities, and this can be used materially to assist the revolution. The concrete results of the red base will be: (1) production in each large college every year of a significant number of students who develop into revolutionary cadres; (2) production in each large college every year of a red mass of students—several hundreds or even thousands of students who reject bourgeois ideology and culture, and who can be mobilised for struggle at any time inside or outside the education sector; (3) premises and facilities in colleges which can be taken over when required for revolutionary activity of any kind; (4) colleges which can be centres of ideological research, servicing of the working-class movement, helping it to develop along the path of revolution; and (5) most importantly the fact that the university or college with a red strategic majority can function as a revolutionary political presence or *foco*, concretely expressing the ideas of socialist revolution to which the working class must be won.

Finally, Anthony Barnett saw it in these terms: "First and foremost the mass of students liberated from the clutches of the authorities. . . . Second, the militant students won over to the revolution. . . . Third, the vanguard organically linking itself with the mass of students. . . . Red bases for the future overthrow of the ruling class and the immediate liberation of the students—that is the goal of the student movement."

There is considerable difficulty in working out what all this actually means in practice. It could mean a long occupation in which some of the students say they are revolutionaries. In a RSSF newsheet entitled *News from the Red Bases* the red bases were no more than groups of RSSF supporters. Despite the evangelical intentions of the authors in the direction of the working class, they themselves admitted, whether red bases existed or not, that the actual contacts with the working class were limited.

On one matter the exponents were clear, and that was the counter-revolutionary nature of students unions. Anthony Barnett referred to them as the "*invisible occupation of the student body by the authorities*, sometimes called guilds, which exactly characterises their pretence at providing the facilities for an apprenticeship subordinated to a master . . . a banal yet effective transplant from the Oxbridge tradition into a more utilitarian milieu. They generate between students the tyranny of unwritten prestige that dominates all university life. . . . Abolish the union." It is difficult to take Barnett seriously at this point, for he argues that unions should be replaced by popular assemblies with a chairman elected from the floor of the meeting, working committees and a sabbatical secretary. This arrangement bears a strong similarity to the students' union he would have just destroyed. Does he not think that when the euphoria of "revolution" had died away and participation in mass meetings was not quite at the former level, the students would seek more permanent structures, recognition by the university, and most probably automatic membership? At Hornsey and Guildford Colleges of Art his dictum was obeyed and the students then spent a year, among other things, reconstructing their unions. If Barnett had been successful he would have saved the Tory Government the job of producing a Consultative Document two and a half years later.

The major argument against the red base is, however, that it could never exist in any meaningful sense in any college. The term is borrowed from quite different contexts, the Chinese Revolution in particular. A red base was a liberated area of countryside, having its own government, armed forces and producing its own food and other commodities. The RSSF red base just does not measure up to this. The term "ideas factory" may appeal to some. So, too, the production of knowledge and ideology for the working class. But this does not mean that a sit-in becomes a red base. Where are the troops, the workers and the peasants? They were not in the universities in 1968.

It is sheer folly to assume that the state would ever allow universities and colleges to become "liberated areas". Fernbach says that "a politically mobilised mass of students can force major concessions from the authorities, and if these concessions are the only way of keeping higher education in production, they will be granted". This is true as far as the everyday practice of militant action by the student movement is concerned, but if the action really involved a "red base", Fernbach would be guiding the students on a thoroughly false prospectus. There would be no concessions—as Che Guevara's experience shows. The possibility of repression is indeed recognised, and the students are offered the following solace: "But given the revolutionaries are serious, this only intensifies the struggle without resolving it. Moreover, it exacerbates the tendency for the struggle to spill over from students to the working class while destroying the liberal façade of the bourgeois state that is the most plausible justification of late capitalism." Here is clearly seen the germ of provocative tactics. Provoking the state into action will itself cause the working class to rise. These politics are dangerous because they give the hand to reaction. Indeed, provocation is a tactic the ruling class itself uses. It is a thoroughly risky business and does not lead to the successful outcome of disputes, still less revolution. On the contrary it leads to defeat and disillusion. Go on, go on, the working class is behind you (somewhere), students are told—the rhetoric which cloaks defeat!

Thankfully, the adventure of the red bases was largely a matter of words.

*The Conservative Party*

The Federation of Conservative Students is the largest student political organisation in the country. The FCS leadership claims a membership in the colleges and universities of 10,000. This is obtained by aggregating together all the memberships of the individual associations and local societies. There is every reason to believe this figure to be entirely notional, for the Conservative Party has a high proportion of inactive members amongst students and other sections of society. Many join the Young Conservatives and Conservative

Associations in the colleges for social reasons—"to play ping pong and look for a mate". A significant number in other circumstances would be Liberals. The FCS differs from other student political organisations in its lower level of activism. It is well patronised by Tory leaders. The political motive of the Tory leadership is probably that they regard the FCS and student politics generally as a useful recruiting ground for future MP's. Certainly the FCS has more than its share of ambitious young men.

There is some evidence to think that the FCS wishes to change from being a political nursery and a social club. An interview conducted by Geoffrey Middleton for the NUS magazine *Magnus* in 1973 indicated that the FCS were going to launch a major bid for the leadership of the student movement. Certainly the number of youth organisers appointed by Central Office has increased in the recent period. Regardless of this, the FCS prides itself on its ability to be in touch with Tory governments and to influence them, to have tea with the PM or get close to the ministerial ear. The FCS thinks that it is a representative body of students—every bit as much as the NUS, if not more so. It likes to speak up for what it conceives to be "moderate" student opinion with the implication that the majority of students hold Tory views. This self-appointed role shows considerable political conceit. The FCS is not the NUS, it merely represents the Conservative students. At the back of the Conservative mind is the belief that they, by virtue of being part of or associated with the ruling class, have a right to be the Government, or are *ipso facto*, representative.

Conservative Associations and societies play a negative role in relation to the development of a mass movement. They in principle oppose the use of direct action, though on a number of occasions the seriousness of a dispute with a college authority has forced them to support these kind of actions. Given the uncommitted nature of much of their membership there is always a more left-inclined section. At the height of the first LSE dispute in 1967 the newly elected President of the Students' Union, Peter Watherston, a Conservative, supported the use of direct action.

The FCS stands for a grants policy much in line with the NUS and wishes to see more priority given to student housing. Its support excludes politics—it thinks the NUS should be "non-political", particularly when there is a Tory government. But one student issue above all marks it out. This is how student unions should be organised and financed. The FCS wishes to see them subject to the powers of a specially appointed Registrar. When they argued for this in 1972 they went directly against the view of the overwhelming majority of students. It is difficult to explain the reasons for FCS support for the Registrar except in terms of Tory authoritarianism, for a Registrar would undermine the autonomy and the representativity of student unions—turning them ultimately into state controlled agencies. In general Conservatives do not do very well in student union elections, and their policies presented to mass meetings gain little support from students. This lack of success is perhaps part of the reason why they think student unions are "unrepresentative".

The Conservative Party has an ambivalent attitude towards students. On the one hand there is a sympathy with youthful idealism. Kenneth Lewis, MP, in his pamphlet *Students in Revolt* said that "student turmoil is a natural feature of our time". Edward Heath at the 1968 NUS Easter Conference said he understood these things—he had visited Republican Spain in the 1930's. Heath also said on this occasion that what students wanted was a good degree and a job with prospects. Tories see students as future Tory voters, presumably because a large number of their parents vote Tory. At the same time, there is another strand of opinion running through the Tory Party. Authoritarianism leads Tories to say that the "students should know their place" and that if they don't, "the young puppies should be put down". This relates to the antipathy towards the left wing and communists. Monday Club elements are notorious for their anti-student views and for believing "more means worse". Favourites (like hanging) with such elements have always been the removal of grants from student demonstrators and the requirement that all students should sign a good behaviour pledge before being allowed into college.

# 6

## PERSPECTIVES AND POLICIES

In this last chapter a perspective for policy and action will be set out. It will not be very detailed, rather it will outline the main directions of possible advance. Much directly relates to the National Union of Students. It is partly a collation of the most important policies and experience, and partly my own view of future priorities. The policies and strategies must be seen in a wide political context. Progress by the student movement on questions of student rights and educational reform is possible only to a limited degree without wider support. Educational expenditure is being severely limited. Notwithstanding the election of a Labour Government there is on the part of the ruling class and its adherents and instruments a growing trend towards reaction, repression and an onslaught on the position and rights of the working class. As recent campaigns and actions have demonstrated, students do not and cannot stand above or aside from these developments, for their own position has been subject to similar attacks. Advance on any one student front, though not determined completely by the overall political situation, is substantially related to the strength of and the advances made by the Labour and progressive movement as a whole. The important point is unity on a mass basis. Students are not entirely dependent for their successes on the Labour movement (any more than the vanguardist converse proposition is true). Both are dependent on unity inside and outside their own ranks.

The chapter will be divided into two parts. The first sets out policies and actions on educational matters, and the second specifically concerns itself with the present problems and perspectives for student organisations and the student movement generally.

I

EDUCATIONAL ISSUES

## 1. Student financing

As at present, student grants are means-tested on parental income; grants are predominantly available only to students with two "A" level GCE's or equivalent qualifications on full-time degree courses; their value is subject to substantial erosion as a result of inflation; sexual discrimination is applied, particularly against married women students; grants are not sufficient to meet a student's maintenance costs for the whole course, so that vacation and/or part-time work becomes obligatory for the overwhelming majority of students; and countless small anomalies exist to plague the individual student, particularly those on lower level courses and those studying at a postgraduate level.

These features of the present grants system are rarely articulated or defended by its proponents and administrators, for to do so would not confer much credit to the system among a wider audience, let alone amongst the students. As against this present system, the student body has to counterpose the objectives for which it will fight. And they must be consolidated in legislation where necessary.

These objectives are:

1. All students by virtue of their adult status and legal independence should receive the full rate of grant regardless of parental circumstance. In order to prevent this causing a subsidy being given to rich parents as a result of the continuation of the Dependant Child Allowance for students in full-time education, fiscal means should be found to ensure that such parents should contribute relatively more to the exchequer than they do now. Students below the age of majority should receive a standardised grant at a lower level—perhaps the living-at-home main rate.

2. All students accepted on to a course of higher or further education should receive financial support at nationally standardised rates. This may take the form of wages paid to students on sandwich courses or on

day or block release. In addition it is imperative that students studying for qualifications on a part-time basis should obtain grant support and/or, at the very least, the remission of tuition fees. Part-time student grants should be made *pro rata* with full time student grants, according to the number of hours a week studied. Equally important is the financial situation of students on non-degree level courses which are full-time—ONC, HNC and "O"/"A" level courses in further education. It is not suggested that all full-time students should receive grants at the same rate—that a student undertaking "O" levels at 17 years should get the same as a postgraduate student in his middle twenties. The primary distinction should rest upon the age of the students rather than the level of course, as at present. The argument that a student must pass through a number of "academic hoops" before being eligible or "safe" enough to receive a full-time grant is objectionable. Students should receive grants when they are accepted on to a course. If a student drops out of a course or fails a crucial assessment his grant should cease, notwithstanding there being proper appeal procedures and provision for re-sits.

3. Students should receive grants for the full duration of their courses. This will mean a substantial improvement in the provision of vacation grants. At present it is not possible for many students to study in the vacations (when often it would be academically desirable for them to do so). The question of the suitability of certain forms of employment as experience counting towards the final assessment of a course, needs to be further investigated.

4. All grants should have a stable value from year to year. The Government in consultation with the NUS and LEA's should establish a cost of living index (indices) for students which will allow for variations in the student cost of living to be matched by increased grant levels. All types of grants should be automatically covered by them.

5. All sexual discrimination in the grants system should be removed. In particular this means that married women should receive the same grant as married men.

6. Tuition fees should be paid in respect of all full-time students. Some

students or their parents are still obliged to pay them. Payment of fees, like the receipt of maintenance grant, should not depend on parental income. It is an outdated practice which breaches the principle that education should be provided free out of community or state-borne expenditure. A particularly damaging tendency has arisen in some areas of further education—that fees can be drastically increased in order to save LEA expenditure on its own budgets. Higher fees in the present context mean reduced educational opportunity. In the areas where admission fees are more acceptable—recreational adult education—they should be kept to a minimum. Concerning overseas students, an element of subsidy should be regarded as an important form of international aid. The discriminatory 1967 level should be lowered and rates agreed upon, as a result of international discussion, which do not inhibit the exchange of students and teachers between different countries.

All these principles are essential and provide the basis for a grants system suited to a pattern of post-school education which will begin to induce students into it, rather than, as at present, place barriers in the way of access. Yet, despite their essential common sense, these objectives seem a long way off—because successive governments have sought to restrict expenditure on student support.

Student loans must be opposed in the strongest terms by all available means. Loans would raise a financial barrier in the way of entry to higher education for many working-class students. Repayment would make study most unattractive to many. Given that a loan system, at least at the beginning, would be an optional extra to the grants system (partial or topping up loans), it would force many students not to opt for the loan but rather to choose to study and work concurrently. This would not only place a far greater strain on many students, it would also result in increased failure rates. By reducing the financial independence of the student, loans would discriminate in favour of those who have private means or whose parents are prepared to support their children by giving them money. Loans would in all probability not save the Government very much money. Part loans would mean small amounts of money being loaned to many people at nil or low rates of interest over a long period of time. Any returns would be slow in coming. In addition, the possibly higher wastage rate would mean a reduced return.

Much has been written about NUS grants campaigns; the need for militant tactics, long drawn out campaigning and the crucial importance of securing wider support, particularly from the Labour movement. Specific actions against individual LEA's with poor records; college based strikes over high rents, hall fees, high refectory prices and inadequate demonstrating fees, should all be undertaken. The campaign must have a number of levels—local militancy, national demonstrative action, lobbying and propaganda activities for increased educational opportunity. Student action on its own might be sufficient to prevent a Tory or some other future government introducing a loans system. If advance is to be made on any of the above six principles the campaigning has to be united and militant over a long period of time and enjoy considerable support from the trade unions and the public in general. Ultimately the campaign is about achieving a much higher public identification with and participation in higher education.

The application of the six principles raises further more profound questions about student finance. A more advanced policy, that of student wages, was until recently the policy of the NUS. It ceased to be so because it proved almost impossible to develop a campaign around the demand for a wage. Right-wing student opinion preferred the grant concept with all its charitable connotations. And sections of left and ultra-left students opposed it on the grounds that they thought it predicated that students were workers, something they were ideologically opposed to.

The student wage is, however, the logical and rational policy extension of the six defined principles. The student wage, even if assessed at no higher rate than an adequate level of grant, has a number of social and educational advantages:

(a) The difference between student status and that of a wage or salary earner would be much smaller than it is now both in terms of cash, rights and legal position. This has obvious attractions from the point of view of student rights.

(b) It would render access to the colleges and universities more attractive. Finance is increasingly a barrier to access. Of itself the student wage principle would not throw open the colleges and universities. To have a full effect it would have to be introduced in association with other equally radical measures of democratisation (see later).

(c) A number of employers, e.g., LEA's, which finance teachers on full-time secondment, pay wages or salaries to students. Assuming that it will be increasingly necessary for technological and social reasons that people receive education/re-education and training/re-training throughout their employed lives, a wages system for students would greatly enhance the transfer of students in and out of the colleges and universities. Post-school education must increasingly be seen as *not* restricted to the 16–21 age group. It cannot be seriously argued that periods of retraining should be conducted on the standard rates of student grant.

(d) At present, and with any system of student grants, the student is disadvantaged in relation to social security as he is not credited with insurance contributions. Supplementary benefit, too, is often difficult for students to obtain in vacations. The student grants system has a built-in element of charity which is both objectionable and outdated. Wages would improve this situation.

Although I am firmly in favour of student wages it is difficult to imagine them being introduced in the foreseeable future. Opponents of the wage idea argue that it would mean in practice an "industrialisation" of education—clocking on procedures, work-study methods, etc. Whilst this is not necessarily the case—teaching staff are paid wages and are not subject to such practices—wages do imply a different type of commitment from the student to the educational process. They would be more suited to an educational course combined with work experience, enabling the student to be employed throughout the year. This raises substantial problems which could perhaps only be satisfactorily solved in a socialist economic context. Here, there would not be the contradiction between education and employment, employee and employer, that there is in the capitalist system.

## 2. Assessment and teaching methods

In chapter 2 a critique of current assessment practice was developed. What should student assessment be like? More anarchist inclined sections of student opinion argue that there should be no assessment at all, just as there should be no criteria of admission to the colleges and universities except personal inclination. This argument has a superficial attraction to it, being the most "radical" one, and one that seeks to abolish the "degree factory" altogether. The cynic might say it was merely an excuse for students to have an easy life. But the basic problem is that educational facilities are limited, and that various forms of assessment are the best means of allocating a scarce commodity.

It is not possible for everyone to be educated within existing facilities or those of the foreseeable future. A more powerful argument against the no-selection-no-assessment position is that assessment and education are inextricably bound up together. The student himself cannot be sure that he has done anything worthwhile unless he makes an assessment of what he has achieved. Individuals do not exist in isolation and comment on one's activities by others (with more experience) is essential. Group, social and institutional assessments are equally important to the educational process. Without assessment in some form education becomes a rather purposeless activity or mere amusement.

The crucial question, however, is how examinations are to be reformed. The first point is that the student should be able to choose the assessment techniques used as far as he is concerned. The second is that the range of techniques used should be increased and made more sophisticated by systematic research. The third is that grading should be abolished and replaced by a simple pass-fail distinction. In stating whether a student has passed or failed, the institution and its teachers ought to be able to say a great deal more about the attainments and prospects of the individuals. Tom Fawthorp in his pamphlet *Education or Examination* argued very strongly for a profile system. This would be a series of detailed accounts or folder of the students' progress. Brian Klug in *Pro-Profiles* (NUS 1974) develops many interesting and valuable points. Other possibilities are peer assessment—assessment of students by students, and collective assessments. This last method would be particularly valuable for group projects and activities. Indeed, education is seen too much as a matter of individual performance, apart from or opposed to that of others. A vital part of employment and life in general is co-operative activity. Formal education equips us little for this, except by the reiteration of rather rigid moral norms.

More widely accepted and less radical alternatives to examinations are open book exams (books being allowed in the examination chamber), essay examinations (where the student knows the question beforehand), extended examinations (where the student is allowed an unlimited period of time and access to literature in order to answer questions), objective tests (where questions asked require yes/no answers), orals and vivas. Forms of assessment which differ from examinations completely are also regarded as alternatives: continuous assessment, theses, dissertations and research projects. Not only is student choice essential but also students must have a say in determining the boundaries of choice. This means student representation at every level of institutional government and a positive effort by college authorities to involve students in innovations of assessment techniques.

The strength of student feelings on the matter, the weight of argument in favour of reform and the misgivings of a large number of teachers, have laid the basis for reform. Of particular value in future will be the statement which was negotiated between the National Union of Students and the three teacher's unions in higher education (despite the fact that it was not fully endorsed by all the parties). This stated that:

   (i) all staff and students should be made aware of the objectives of the course and the methods of assessment used (the methods of assessment to relate to the educational objectives);

  (ii) students should know when they are being assessed, e.g., if attendance at lectures or performance in seminars is being included;

 (iii) assessment should be seen as a separate activity from grading; assessment must be seen as an essential and integral part of a teacher's responsibilities and his workload adjusted accordingly;

 (iv) there should be a reasonable spacing between examination papers—no more than one three-hour paper or practical per 24 hours;

  (v) a clear appeals procedure should be established to minimise error;

 (vi) all institutions of higher and further education should accept the principle of automatic re-sit in the event of failure;

(vii) the student should be notified privately of the results of his examination and there should be no public display of failure.

These and the other proposals mentioned provide many opportunities for progress to be made. Much needs to be done if the "degree factory" is to be completely vanquished.

Teaching methods like assessment techniques are integrally related to the aims and objectives of courses. Emphasis on the lecture method goes hand in hand with reliance on formal examinations. Lectures will tend to be the predominant teaching method if a prime educational objective is the imparting of facts. If on the other hand one of the educational objectives is to promote enquiry and participation, then there will be less reliance on the lecture method. From the student point of view, despite the 1965 Hale Report on university teaching methods and the Brynmor-Jones Report on audio-visual aids in scientific education making generally progressive recommendations, change has been all too slow.

The specific problems are:

(i) A disproportionate emphasis is placed on research performance and publication, or on competence in administration, in the assessment of a teacher's suitability for appointment and promotion. Teaching abilities are secondary criteria. From the student point of view the two should be given equal emphasis. The danger of the present situation is that senior academics tend to be indifferent or disinterested teachers. This sets the tone for the teaching force in higher education generally. Even in the colleges of education, ability to teach in the higher education context is not given due weight. It is assumed that the good teacher of primary age children will be a good teacher in the college context. This is not so.

(ii) The undue weight given to the lecture acts as a brake on educational innovation. Undoubtedly for most students in higher education the seminar and tutorial are preferable teaching methods. This does not mean that the lecture should be removed altogether. A well-prepared lecture with an imaginative use of audio-visual aids can be a valuable and efficient teaching method. The NUS conducted a survey into teaching methods in higher education in 1969, taking a sample of students in eight different higher educational institutions. This revealed that 55 per cent of the respondents had no tutorials at all. As it was ten, twenty and thirty years ago, British students are over-lectured.

Although there has been a policy shift of emphasis away from the lecture, in practice it continues as the main method because lecturers have not been trained to teach in other ways. Unless opposition is widespread there can be little hope of improvement in teaching methods in the next decade because of the Government's intention of increasing staff-student ratios. Fewer staff teaching the same number of students will mean a greater reliance on the lecture. It will be particularly difficult for those students undertaking courses, such as the two-year Diploma in Higher Education, which are supposed to embody flexibility and wider educational choice. With relatively fewer staff this will be virtually impossible.

(iii) Most lecturers in higher and further education are not professionally trained. This is largely due to the educational deadweight of the British academic tradition; possession of knowledge and academic proficiency is assumed to mean the cognoscenti can teach as well. Until quite recently the case for professional training was unrecognised. It is now largely accepted, though very little has been done about it. Some universities think that a week's induction for new lecturers at the beginning of the academic year is sufficient. This is a dangerous illusion designed to foster complacency. Compulsory training for all new entrants (including into teacher education) and periodic in-service training is necessary. This is what is required for school teachers and the same principle should apply in higher and further education. Students have as many specialised educational needs as schoolchildren. The Government sets an atrocious example. The Russell Report in 1966 recommended compulsory training for all new teachers in further education. The Labour Government rejected this. The Tory Government's White Paper (December 1972) said it "wished to see initial training become more widespread" but doubted "whether it would be desirable to impose compulsory initial training on a category of teachers (such as those intending to teach mainly in the 16–19 age group) which could not be easily defined in advance". On the contrary the 16–19 age group is as definable as 11–16 or 5–11. But then the Government, barely after there was a compulsory requirement for all graduates entering school teaching to be trained, waived it for mathematics teachers on the bogus grounds that training inhibits entry to the profession. Students and the teachers unions want improved training provision. Yet it is one of those "frills" that at the first sign of economic difficulty the Government and college authorities will chop.

(iv) Students wish to comment constructively on the teaching methods that are used. In general there has been an improvement in the formal arrangements for student participation in this area. But because of the inadequate funds and priority given to professional training and the absence of structures and procedures to "enable" teachers to improve their teaching, the exercise has not proved as valuable as it could have been. It is all very well for students and enthusiastic staff to make radical recommendations. Action is a different matter. The dictates of "academic freedom" allow the individual teacher to do what he wants in front of the students.

The conclusion of the foregoing is that there has been the recognition of the need for changes. But inadequate funds and structural inertia in the colleges and universities have meant that change has been slow. There seems no reason to think that it will be any quicker in future. Students need to become angrier about these matters.

### 3. Access and entry qualifications

Access to higher and, to a lesser extent, further education is biased against working-class sections of the populations. It is selective according to performance in school-leaving examinations. Although a rapid expansion has taken place in the last decade the social composition of the student body is much as it was pre-Robbins. Any radical perspective must have as its objective the raising of educational opportunity for the overwhelming majority who at present have no access to post-school education and no educational provision made for them. At present there are two aspects to the problem—the policies of particular institutions (particularly the universities) and longer term matters.

Different universities have widely varying entrance requirements for the same degree courses. Some universities are not prepared to accept woodwork and metalwork as suitable "A" levels. This can mean that students with equal qualifications at "A" level have varying chances of access, a problem which is particularly evident in universities which have rigid departmental structures and separate entrance requirements for different departments. The history of the B.Ed. degree is a notorious example of this inequality and arbitrariness. The variations in the practice of different universities—emphasis placed on "A" level results in the selection of students on to the B.Ed., the differences of classification and grading and the proportions of certificate students able to stay on for an additional year—bear no relationship to the competence of students or the professional needs of teachers in the different areas covered by the universities' validation.

The universities adopt a very ambiguous attitude towards the qualifications provided by further education. An NUS report in 1969 described the situation as follows: "The universities of Aston, Brunel, Bath, Bradford, City, Hull, Sussex, Newcastle, Heriot-Watt, Surrey, UWIST and Salford accept passes in appropriate subjects at high standard in ONC, OND, HNC and HND in lieu of GCE ordinary level and advanced level passes. Southampton accepts ONC and OND with distinction in mathematics in lieu of advanced level GCE. The universities of Leeds, Sheffield, Liverpool, Cardiff, Manchester, Birmingham, Swansea and Ulster will accept as equivalent to an advanced level GCE pass (for entry on to a three-year course) a subject passed at HNC or HND; or a subject passed at 60 per cent or better at main or subsidiary standard in ONC or OND (for entry to a four-year degree course)."

The situation is even more variable for mature entrants. The colleges of education have in recent years been quite successful in attracting mature entrants for teachers' certificate courses, though in many cases this has meant that the students have had to study for the requisite GCE's at technical colleges part-time or by correspondence. Yet the universities, with the notable exceptions of Birkbeck College and the Open University, have ignored this problem—less than 5 per cent of university entrants are mature students. Their equivocal attitude towards ONC, OND qualifications is particularly reprehensible. These courses are not at all the soft option that the universities assume. They are two-year courses with quite rigorous standards. Universities are educational institutions designed to recruit students direct from school sixth forms. This and the reliance on "A" level passes is the main reason for their highly selective access. The polytechnics and the colleges of education for their part are showing every sign of imitating this.

The long-term problem is the overall reform of university entrance requirements. Various attempts have been made in recent years to secure change. These have been unsuccessful because school teachers and the universities have never been able to agree. The universities have sought to preserve their "subject in depth" approach, itself resting on a rigid departmentalism and segregation of different areas of knowledge. As a result it has not been possible to reform the sixth form curriculum in a general direction—away from single subject in depth study and the highly dangerous early specialisation this entails. The stranglehold of university entrance requirements has become progressively worse in the last thirty years. Prior to the war the ratio of passes at Higher School Certificate (the forerunner to "A" levels) to entrants to universities was 1 : 2. In 1966 the equivalent ratio was 2 : 1—a shift of 400 per cent. Despite the reluctance of many to defend the "A" level system and the fact that individual universities will attempt reforms, there is every indication that competition will become even sharper.

What proposals for reform need to be implemented?


(i) At present students applying for courses in different sectors of higher education apply through different agencies—the UCCA for universities, a central registry scheme for colleges of education and a DES-run service for further education and the polytechnics. This limits the student's options. It reflects a rigid binary status distinction between the different institutions. A greater flexibility and wider range of choice would be promoted by having one central clearing house for processing all applications.


(ii) Improved counselling in schools and further education establishments about the choices available in higher education would assist students considerably. The "gap" between school and higher education institutions is still very wide and students do not receive enough assistance in bridging it. Present levels of specialisation require the student to receive very good advice. The premature choices that many students are forced to take means that some will subsequently desire to study different subjects than those they originally specialised in at school. In addition, deferred entry to higher education, years out between the years of a course and voluntary service or relevant employment, are all matters on which students could be better advised.

The counselling necessary could be run in association with the central clearing house and the existing youth employment service.

(iii) Colleges and universities must broaden their entry requirements. There can never be a significant widening of educational opportunity with the present over-reliance on "A" levels; too many of the age group will always leave school prior to taking GCE's. Further education will never be able to provide all who leave with the requisite "A" levels. It should not attempt to do so. Most particularly it is necessary for ONC/OND, HNC/HND qualifications to be regarded as equivalent to "A" levels (and a "one for one" year exemption for HND holders). This must also apply for any new diploma in higher education. Equally important is a liberalisation of the admission requirements in respect of mature students. With the Open University showing that many without formal academic qualifications can satisfactorily complete a degree course (under very difficult circumstances), there can be no educational reason for other institutions holding on to restrictive positions. Universities and polytechnics should admit mature students on lower academic qualifications and regard work experience as equivalent to educational achievement.

(iv) The rigidity of existing higher education courses and the consequent wastage due to students being unable to transfer can be partly overcome by students being admitted for one of a number of courses in the polytechnic or university. General rather than specific course-orientated admission requirements would be a valuable reform. In a longer term it should be possible to admit students to the institution *first* and the course *second* as tends to be done in non-advanced further education. This would ameliorate some of the harmful aspects of the "A" level system. Ultimately the objective should be to design courses for students rather than students for courses, as is largely the case at present.

(v) "A" levels will have to be abolished. In what has been written about student assessment, radical demands for a profile system have been made. Admission, the assessment of progress during a course and the final statement of achievement, are all part of the same general process. Reform should be consistent throughout. A profile based on previous educational performance and activities is a possible means of determining admission. There may be some improvement if a single school-leaving examination comes into force. Two principles should apply. Sufficient options should be available for students to give them more choice in determining the nature of their courses. Institutions of higher education should positively attempt to attract students and regard it as a failure on their part if a student fails the course. Today the student has little direct control over the course taken, and in the event of failure the student alone is blamed.

The question of broadening access is not simply a matter of reforming entry qualifications. It relates to the totality of higher and further education. Attitudes of staff and their expectations for students at all levels are underpinned by notions of selection based in part on their own (selected) educational experience. Status attitudes held by students, parents and society in general are based on selection and the presumed ability of only a few to do well in higher education. This is bolstered up by and reciprocally interrelated to the grants system, which only rewards reasonably those that have "gone through the hoops". Finally come the staffing and salary structures of post-school education. The differentials between universities and public sector colleges are well known. Less known is that in further education, an area which is supposed to be most responsive to the educational "under-achievers", similar barriers and discrimination exist. According to the Burnham Further Education report, courses are classified $A_1$, $A_2$, B and C, according to level—$A_1$ is degree level, C below "O" level. In calculating staff establishment, both numbers and levels of staff appointments, colleges measure up to points totals. One student hour on a degree course counts over three times that of a "C" grade student. Thus staff salaries, promotion and staff-student ratios relate directly to academic level. This can only be seen as discrimination against those without formal academic qualifications. Attitude and status go hand in hand with money and entrance requirements. The whole system has to be reformed and in some respects the status and points system turned upside down. The same problem exists in the schools, with primary school and "lower stream" children and their teachers being disadvantaged.

I consider that if the working class is to secure equal access to post-school education these specifically educational and administrative measures may well be insufficient. Certainly there will have to be a massive expansion of provision and student places. Even this may not be enough and special quota arrangements may have to be considered as a short-term measure, with the colleges and universities systematically thrown open to the education of working-class young people (notwithstanding equally important measures regarding school curricula, financing and teaching). This is what happened in Poland and the German Democratic Republic in the late 1940's and early 1950's.

### 4. The government of colleges and universities

The inadequacies of existing student representation and the changing situation in the colleges has led to four strategies and theoretical approaches within the student body. First, there are those who are broadly satisfied with the existing token representation. Secondly, there is the position most consistently advocated by the International Socialists, that having representatives on governing committees is tantamount to identification with the decisions of the committee. It is argued that the student unions contradict their basic purpose by becoming part of the running of the college or participating in "rationalisation measures which seek to solve the crises of higher education at the students' expense". Another variant is that student unions and the NUS should not seek representation at national or local level on government advisory committees, as this would mean absorption into the capitalist state machine. There are many nuances of approach here, but all lead to the conclusion that student representation is to be abandoned or reduced to observer status only—so that "intelligence about the enemy's operations" can be garnered. This is styled as a "trade union approach"—conducting relations with college authorities solely on the basis of formal communication, negotiation or confrontation.

Of this second approach it may be said that, while it is valid to consider withdrawal from representation as a tactic in certain circumstances, to withdraw totally is to play right into the hands of the authorities. They didn't want student representation in the first place. The approach is in addition based on a very simplistic conception of the educational institutions—that they are mere appendages of the state or that they can be likened directly to an industrial enterprise. Both assertions ignore the nature of education and the practical value of student representation as a mechanism of seeking reform in the students' interest. A straightforward us/them attitude poses teachers against students in a mirror image of the authoritarian model, that students come to college to learn and that teachers teach them as passive recipients. This completely ignores developments towards participation and more progressive teaching techniques.

The third strategy is similar to the "trade union approach" as a strategy of withdrawal, but diverges by proposing a completely different pattern of government for the colleges which, it is said, should be based on the principle of one man one vote for all staff, students and auxiliary staff of the institution. There are a number of variants:

(i) The student power approach, that students should run the colleges and universities in totality, hire and fire staff, etc.

(ii) That the student union should expand its membership and run the college through general meetings, now called general assemblies.

(iii) That students, staff and workers should elect the governing body and other major committees of the institution by ballot.

The first of these variants was put forward as a principle by some members of the RSA in 1966; the second was attempted through the Association of Members of the Hornsey College of Art in the 1968 occupation; and the third was borrowed from the policy of the Finnish National Union of Students (SYL).

These strategies have a democratic appearance, but are based on principles which must be challenged. In the first place, the result would be a relative isolation of the institution from the community—a diminution of external representation in the running of the colleges. In one sense this is a regression to the Oxbridge and medieval Italian pattern of the self-governing community of scholars. To be effective, moreover, any scheme of mass meetings and regular direct democracy requires a very high and continuous level of involvement and interest, which is not always the case. The proposals smack of the sit-in and are an attempt to transplant wholesale the mores of this activity into the rules of the institution—or to regard the practices of the student union as superior to any other.

In the second place, one may ask whether all educational questions can ever be satisfactorily solved by mass meeting. The mass meeting is only one (very important) way of arriving at decisions. Perhaps the most basic assumption is that staff and students are equivalent (one member of staff equals one student). But this would mean a radical alteration in the status of staff, their future position becoming one of similarity to students. But is there no difference? Teachers are the people designated to teach the students, and in this capacity have an importance in the colleges and universities which far outweighs their numbers. The proponents of a "general meeting" system may argue that such individuals would always be able to exert a substantial influence on the proceedings by virtue of their knowledge and powers of persuasion. But this is not necessarily the case. And should students, as the majority, have full control over what is taught in the colleges and universities when they are largely publicly financed? I think not.

The fourth strategy, by comparison, is based on the concept of constituency, that students and staff have separate, complementary and equal roles to play in the running of the institution. To these two are added those of administrative staff, ancillary workers and, most importantly, external social interests. All need to be represented in institutional government to varying degrees. At the moment students are under-represented, junior staff are under-represented to a lesser extent, and there is a need for a more democratic and popular representation of external social interests. Complementary to this is the view that educational questions should be under joint student-staff control, that residences and other student amenities should be under the control of students, and that union organisations of staff and students have the right to autonomy. The strategy of this position is to attempt to strengthen the basis of student representation already established by attacking particular evident weaknesses and advocating more comprehensive schemes of democratisation. It seeks to use representation to achieve positive reforms of benefit to students. The advantage of this general approach is its practicality. It avoids the complacency of the first approach, the barrenness and crudity of the second and the anarchistic idealism of the third.

Students are inadequately represented in college and university government. College authorities, as in the mid-1960's, are taking decisions contrary to the wishes of students. Students feel that their rights are not being properly protected and representation offers a mechanism through which something can be done. It is, moreover, necessary to reassert the principle that administrative questions must be subservient to educational and policy matters. In general administrative procedures can simplified and made more adaptable so as to be more widely understood.

The following may, then, be put forward as medium-term and long-term objectives:

(a) Student representation needs to be extended and strengthened at all levels of institutional government. Token representation, joint consultative committees, reserved areas, the exclusion of student representatives and non-voting status will have to be dealt with. In particular, colleges and universities will have to accept that students have a role to play in appointing staff. Such decisions are arguably the most important and student representation cannot be fully effective unless it impinges on this area. It is difficult to develop and apply specific formulas about the quantity of student representation that should apply in different areas, committees or representative assemblies. Rigid formulas of proportionality 50:50 or 60:40 tend to remove the possibility of negotiation on an institutional basis.

(b) There must be a marked extension of the involvement of popular interest in the running of higher education establishments. All too often representatives of external interests are pliant supporters of the Principal or Vice-Chancellor and of the spokesmen of the employers or other corporate interests. Trade union organisations, community bodies, tenants' and residents' associations are under-represented or not represented at all. The form of this representation will vary according to the extent the college draws its students from the immediate locality, the extent of its specialisation and other factors. The members of the governing bodies must not sit simply as individuals, as tends to be the case at present. They have two responsibilities: in a corporate sense to superintend the affairs of the college *and* to represent and report to those they represent. Unless there is this representation a local community cannot fully identify with and support the institution.

Democratisation must be seen in relation to the degree of freedom the teachers and students should have. The responsibility for overall policy must be given to the college and vested in a board of governers on which there should be substantial external and democratic representation. Subject to this, academic matters should be the prerogative of students and staff. Academic freedom does not, as many argue, exist in a vacuum, divorced from wider social and economic considerations. It has customarily meant the freedom of the academic (professor) to profess what he likes. It has not meant that teachers elsewhere in post-school education or students have an equivalent prerogative. If academic freedom is to be defended on free speech grounds its definition must be broadened to include the same rights for other teachers and students, freedom of access to all members of the population and democratic internal government of the institutions. Unless this is the case academic freedom is an indefensible minority or professorial privilege more like academic dictatorship in practice. Given the increasing desirability of radical social change in Britain, how should curricula change to meet this new situation? Primarily this should not occur as a result of direction from without, though clearly any government has both a political and administrative responsibility for the development of the educational system as a whole. It should develop from the activities of the student movement and changed attitudes amongst staff. The defence of the principle that unpopular and unconventional opinions should be expressed by individuals within the academic and educational context does not mean that the institution can stand above society. New staff appointments and courses should reflect changing circumstances, but academic competence must remain a primary consideration in staff appointments.

(c) Student representation must be conducted with the two procedural principles of mandation and accountability. The student body, or sections of it, has the responsibility to set out the principles of its position on matters of major importance. Representatives then have to adhere to this and advocate it as skilfully as they are able. This does not mean that representatives in committee merely rehearse positions prepared elsewhere. This is how representation is portrayed by its opponents, those who are incapable of seeing a committee function as anything but a confidential law unto itself. Accountability is equally important. Student representatives must report to those whom they represent. Without this the students have no knowledge of what has been decided, still less whether what they wanted has been secured. In the process of taking account the behaviour of the representatives should also be assessed.

(d) Given the strengthening of student representation in college government it is essential that student unions take a greater lead than they have done so far. Representatives cannot be left alone to fend for themselves. They have to be serviced, organised and co-ordinated. Unless this is done the impact of representation is dissipated; individuals can be incorporated into a structure and end up representing the institution to the students. The union must also ensure that democratic practices are adhered to and where possible itself supervise and organise the election of student representatives.

(e) Representation must never be seen, except in strategic and tactical terms, as an end in itself. Too many union officers see it as a question of communication or merely sitting on the appropriate committee. The purpose of representation is to secure educational and institutional change. Reform of government must go hand in hand with democratisation of access.

Democratisation of college government must be a central objective of the student movement. Ultimately the goal is the creation of a totally different nature of authority which will stem from the wishes of students and staff and wider popular concern. It will not stand over students but with them, they will form an integral part of that authority. This clearly has a democratic and radical implication for society in general.

## 5. *The curriculum and the objectives of education*

The following are guidelines for activity and should be read in connection with what has already been written in chapter 2:

(i) The principle of *relevance*. Despite the over-use and misuse of the word, it conveys a kernel of value. Courses should be related to the needs and problems of the majority of people, not commercial profit, rapid career advancement or the niceties of Academe. The concept of community-related curricula has been formulated. This means the incorporation of social practical problems into curricula as a vital part of a student's education. In practice this idea would mean a considerable extension of the sandwich course principle. The contradictory aspects and those which would attack student circumstances and impoverish education need to be faced squarely.

(ii) Recognition of the *false contradiction* between academic and vocational courses. Both academic and vocational type courses are often too specialised. Academically specialised courses are vocational in that they inculcate the expectation (and the reality for a small number) of an academic/research career. The real alternative to academic and abstruse courses is not to replace them with an intense employment orientation, but the institution of broader based courses with a multiplicity of options and choices for students.

(iii) The principle that a fundamental part of any higher or further education course is the exercise of *student choice*. Choices have to be made on graduation and many times throughout a lifetime's employment. Exercising judgement about educational options is an excellent way of learning this capacity. As important as choosing is the actual choice and participation of students in the development of new courses (choices). I believe that unit-based courses *combined* with adequate and expert counselling and participatory discussion offer the best opportunities. An aspect of course and curricular criticism that has shown signs of developing in recent years is the compilation of alternative prospectuses. These are drawn together by groups of students under the aegis of the students' union. The idea is that students should through this medium express their authoritative view of what the courses are like. Thereby it aims at "cutting through" the official PR prospectus and tries to tell applicant students what the place is really like.

Yet it is possible to build a wide variety of options into more conventional linear and branched courses. Project work must form an integral part of all courses.

Some argue that a good means of dealing with the problem of over-specialisation in the school curriculum and assisting students to satisfactorily bridge the difference between school and higher education is deferred entry. Students should spend a year or two between school and college at work, on voluntary service, or abroad, so as to gain experience which will broaden the outlook on life. This idea has a number of attractions and equally obvious disadvantages. It has been suggested that the one or two years should be compulsory and take the form of "substitute national service". Some hanker for conscription as a means of dealing with the problems of youth. Without doubt deferred entry would broaden the outlook of many. Yet it might result in a considerable difficulty for the student getting back to the life of study. It might cause more students to fail early on in their courses. Perhaps more serious is the situation for working-class students. Experience of work and the higher income this provides compared with the grant might tip the scales against entry. Similarly, marriage and parenthood will limit opportunities for women. Certainly it is desirable that there should be a greater mature student access to higher education. But this is a pipe dream unless grant levels compare favourably with wage and salary levels. Unless moves are made in this direction the deferred entry could be a means of "weeding out those who don't really want higher education", that is to say, reducing access. Certainly the student movement can have no truck with compulsory deferred entry. The real problem is course structures and curricular content.

(iv) The principle that the *objectives* of a course should be clear and capable of discussion, challenge and modification. The objectives of the course are more important than curricular content. I believe that the following educational objectives are most important in the immediate context: the development of powers of critical thought, the ability to take decisions, the capacity for students to work individually *and* in groups, and the acquisition of certain types of skills and knowledge. The first three are more important than the last.

(v) The need to isolate and contest the *ideological* and socio-political premises which underlie the objectives of courses. This is easier in the social sciences where the questions of Marxism, the socialist countries, trade unions, and a wide range of other political matters are explicitly part of the curriculum. In natural and applied sciences the major question may be at one remove—the uses and abuses of the content of science and who benefits from its application. Jonathan Slack in "Class Struggle Among the Molecules" (in *Counter Course: a Handbook for Course Criticism*) recalls the ideological influences in the school organic chemistry curriculum and quotes from a textbook he was provided:

"Perspex's outstanding quality is its clarity, which gives objects made from it a brilliant and beautiful appearance. It is used for making the hoods and gun turrets of military aircraft."

Left-wing and radical groups of students can do much to expose and contest the reactionary premises of many course objectives. Such activities must not end at discussion. Concrete proposals for change, and action where appropriate to back them up, are necessary. The objective should be to secure reform. The Communist University of London is another way of tackling this problem in a more political context.

The alternative and free universities that have been established from time to time in local disputes have had variable success. These are both protests and attempts to secure educational change. They involve the setting up of courses (or programmes of lectures) to which lecturers more sympathetic to student points of view are invited. They are designed to show students in general and college authorities what is wrong and how it should be changed. The major attempts were at Essex and LSE in 1967–8.

Student Community Action (SCA) has been one of the main developments in this area. What is it and what has been achieved? A prominent aspect of the student movement's activities in the United States has been Community Action. Here student activists "go out" from the campuses to come to terms with the social problems of particular sections of the population, e.g., SNCC and civil rights activities in the southern states. In Britain established patterns of "do-gooding" voluntary work, the paternalistic Missions of London's East End, came under increasing attacks from activist students in the late 1960's. Rags, Panto, Commemoration Weeks and the like, were designed to collect money for the "needy" in the university's locality, respectable national charities, etc. They were seen as "soup kitchens" designed to paper over the cracks and ameliorate short-term sufferings. Radicals at this time increasingly opposed these annual forays into the community to collect money. They wanted a more permanent and radical relationship. A sit-in over student representation at Birmingham University in December 1968 caused many students to pose questions about their education and its social relationships. This provided the catalyst which initiated national action to change voluntary student work, and place it on a higher and more political level. The intention was to change society rather than end up doing the dirty work for the authorities. Since 1969 the NUS has fostered a national SCA project.

Alan Barr, one of the main architects of the SCA project defined it as follows: "Community action I define as a process in which deprived groups organise themselves to seek redress of grievance by collective political action. It is a process in which the community defines the objectives and the means of action. Student involvement in such activity requires a great deal of skill and long-term commitment. The roles which they perform should support the activities of the local group. For instance, they may produce information or financial resources for the use of the group. When a good relationship has been established between students and local people an advisory role may develop. However, it is my experience that students have more to learn from local community activists than they can contribute" (*Student Community Action*, Bedford Square Press 1972).

The second and equally important aspect has been the promotion or change in the curriculum. Perhaps the student movement overestimated what the SCA could do, for it has not achieved as much as was originally expected. It is easier for many activists to slip into the old "do-gooding" mould—the proverbial "soup for vagrants and decorating old people's homes". This is politically non-contentious and involves no conflict with authority, civil or academic, and can obscure the need for social and political change. It strikes a strong chord in the middle-class mentality. Privilege and guilt is justified by a bit of "slumming" now and again—notwithstanding any positive effect these acts may have and their sincere motivation. Paternalism can take a political form in activists assuming that people have to be organised because they are incapable of doing so themselves. Such paternalism seems to concentrate on the most lumpen and unorganised sections of the population, ignoring the more class-conscious and organised working-class elements. Accordingly the emphasis on the community can assume a non-class approach, a sort of participatory liberalism and enthusiastic populism.

Its very looseness and political heterogeneity is the essence of SCA. It shows some of the weaknesses and strengths of student political activities. The scope of the project in terms of educational reform makes it very important, yet the motley collection of social engineers, do-gooders and ultra-leftists have achieved little more than the production of discussion papers and a network of contacts. Some would say that students are by definition unsuited to social and community work, for success requires many years of patient application.

Perhaps it was too much to expect a radical, organised and coherent plan of action for curricular reform. A number of positive activities have been undertaken and the NUS and student unions have been able to offer their framework to a section of students previously largely estranged from it. Limited (and worthwhile) gains. For the future those involved in SCA and all aspects of student unions must tackle the question of educational and curricular reform with urgency. The social class issues and the question of trade unions must not be shirked by SCA activists. The question "are we bolstering up the existing order?" in the SCA activities must always be posed and answered in the negative. On one thing we can be clear, activities of the NUS in the 1930–40's need to be fully studied.

## 5. *The comprehensive framework*

The word comprehensive has several associated meanings. Comprehensive reorganisation means the institutional changes necessary to remove arbitrary status—distinctions between college and university. An institution, on the other hand, is not comprehensive unless it provides a wide variety of courses in terms of level, depth and subject. Likewise, it refers to access; a college cannot be comprehensive unless the social composition of its student body approximates to that of the population as a whole. Finally, a particular college may not be fully comprehensive but a system of education as a whole can be. Comprehensive reform of the structure and administration of post-school education is urgent. Educational reforms of the type outlined above will be limited if undertaken within the present system. There is no rational allocation of resources in a divided system of post-school education; status distinctions exert a harmful divisive influence inhibiting educational development outside the university sector; competition between the educational institutions is the rule when there should be much more co-operation.

Soon after Mr. Crosland's binary speech in 1965, proposals for comprehensivation were formulated. At first they were concerned almost entirely with the universities and the newly formed polytechnics—colleges of education and non-advanced further education being largely ignored. Professor Pedley persuasively developed a scheme of reorganisation drawing on the experience of secondary reorganisations. The universities were compared to the grammar schools. The NUS was one of the first organisations to support a comprehensive policy, though on rather university biased terms. The formulation developed was the comprehensive university. All institutions were to be amalgamated with existing universities on advantageous terms to the universities. Another scheme developed in 1966 was the quaternary structure. This meant an institutional separation of further from higher education and comprehensive reorganisation either side of the 18-plus line. As the contradictions of the binary system have become more marked so support for reform has grown. Even establishment bodies are now obliged to make sympathetic statements. The Standing Conference of Regional Advisory Councils in a recent report recommended that there should be a "national committee to establish effective co-operation in the planning and development of the whole of higher education". The subcommittee of the Parliamentary Expenditure examining higher and further education in 1973 recommended the creation of a Higher Education Commission "to have overall responsibility for advising the Minister on the financing and administration of the whole higher education sector, and for its planning and co-ordination". The Labour Party's Green Paper on Higher and Further Education published in 1973 recommended the establishment of an Adult Education Commission which would be responsible for the planning and financing of all post-18 adult education. Also in 1973 the ATTI recommended that a National Council for Further and Higher Education should have a planning and administrative role for all post-school education.

There are a number of proposals current. They all embody a measure of comprehensive reorganisation. What should be the principles of any reorganisation?

(i) There can be no omission of the 16–18 age group. Artificial status distinctions between those in further-education colleges and those still at school must be abolished. The matter is certainly not just about degrees, post-eighteen work, the universities, polytechnics and colleges of education. If reorganisation was carried out on this basis alone a new barrier of 18-plus would be created. All post-school, further and adult education work must be dealt with.

(ii) Any national body set up, e.g., the National Council for Further and Higher Education, must be representative of all interests concerned. It must have both planning and administrative powers. However, it should not be a means of removing the political responsibilities of the Secretary of State. The Government must be responsible for the level of expenditure and overall planning considerations.

(iii) There must be a regional framework established to complement the national body. Without this it will be very difficult to co-ordinate and plan the activities of different institutions and sectors. It is possible that the extant Regional Advisory Councils could have their responsibilities widened to allow for superintendence of the universities. Likewise, it must be clear what role the Local Education Authorities are to play. It is not feasible to take all post-school education away from the LEA's. Indeed, as the organs of local government and for a measure of local democracy they have an important role. There has to be a means for a partnership. But higher education must be removed from the public sector and financed under a modified UGC-type structure—the national council referred to in (ii).

(iv) The institutions themselves should be based on amalgamations and developments of the existing colleges and universities. Assuming that access to post-school education will be selective for the foreseeable future, a large measure of differentiation between institutions will be necessary. The important principle in the short term is that the system should be comprehensive and that a full choice can be offered the individual student by appropriate transfer arrangements. It is important not to draw too close an analogy between post-school institutions and some of the new comprehensive schools. Certainly colleges of education must be institutionally amalgamated into the rest of the system. The distinctions between universities and polytechnics and the colleges of education should be progressively overcome. All institutions at present doing advanced work should be allowed to continue to develop it. There must be no "decapitations" of advanced work as happened under the 1956 and 1966 White Papers. Advanced and non-advanced work can profitably coexist in the same institutions.

(v) In order that status distinctions can be satisfactorily overcome it is necessary that all institutions have a similar degree of autonomy in their educational activities. It is undesirable to give chartered (university) status to all colleges and it may be necessary to withdraw and modify the charters of universities in respect of degree-awarding powers. A regional framework of validation, within which the universities could play an important role, is probably the best set-up to give all institutions responsibilities in this important area. Such a regional framework must be separate from the regional administrative and planning framework.

(vi) Given the impossibility and undesirability of removing all post-school education from the purview of the LEA's, there will be a duality of administration, albeit with considerably altered dividing lines. In this situation it is essential that the Government by legislation lays down very clear instruction to LEA's and the National Council for Further and Higher Education to ensure that there is comparability of resources, salary scales for teachers, student grants, etc., otherwise the evils of the present system will re-emerge.

To conclude, the overall perspective must be one of democratisation. The interrelated objectives are: a wider access to post-school education, an integrated system of institutions, enhanced popular and student control over the colleges and universities and a greater educational flexibility favouring student choice. All these changes hang equally on the necessity of a rapid increase in expenditure (and the political decisions which will allow this) and the outlined structural changes.

## II

### STUDENT ORGANISATIONS AND THE STUDENT MOVEMENT

Student unions have been and will remain central to the development of the student movement as a whole. During the last six years they and the NUS have come to occupy an indispensable position. The same will pertain in future. What follows is a consideration of some points of future elevance.

1. *The extension of unionism* is a central task facing the student movement. This must primarily be in further education, the secondary schools, part-time and health services and among other "professional" students. Large sections of the student body are effectively unorganised and unions are largely based in higher education. The difficulties with extending unionism cannot be underestimated. There are a range of problems—college authorities will resist unions in all except their tamest form. Student attitudes in these sectors are often back-ward—either highly vocational ("we're not interested in unions, they're not part of the course") or strongly influenced by authority. Students on short-duration courses pose other problems. Concerning school students there is an urgent need to build branches of the National Union of School Students (NUSS) and for their recognition by school authorities, the right to use facilities and to receive grants. For further education unions the automatic principle for all students must be fully implemented. The unions must be given sufficient financial support to enable them to develop organisation and administration that will overcome the all too common continuity problems.·

The question of autonomy in this sector is not of the same sort as in higher education. Because of the younger age of students, the greater proportion of part-time, day-release and short-course students, it is essential that college authorities and members of staff give assistance. This must not be interference. For part-time students the problems are in many ways so difficult that only a national organisation, with the full support of the NUS, will be capable of dealing with them. Such a body would give assistance to part-time students locally, along with the local student unions, and represent them with the NUS nationally.

At present there are marked discrepancies in provision of union fees and buildings. It is intolerable that students at universities should have larger union buildings and higher subscriptions than those in other sectors of higher education. Although comprehensive reorganisations of post-school education will make an impact on the problem, there must be action by the DES to ensure a measure of standardisation of union fees. As a preliminary method of ensuring greater equality a number of standard union fees (say for degree level, non-advanced and part-time students) could be applied. In addition, uniform provision per unit of student population should be worked out and applied.

For students in the medical and health services co-operation must be developed with the relevant trade unions (unionising the staff which the students will ultimately become). In this context it is difficult to say that the automatic membership principle should apply. Trade union branches of student nurses, student physiotherapists, etc., may be the best way of proceeding. However, they must have a dual orientation—towards the trade unions and towards the NUS. The National Union must give this area a very high priority. The preparation of manuals of guidance, the full establishment of a field officer scheme and the assertion of political priority are all essential.

*2. The widening of the range of student union activities.* Student unions have developed important new areas of activity in recent years—disputes, representation, community action, relations with trade unions, etc. All these relatively new developments must be consolidated. Student unions and the NUS must be dynamic organisations. They must continually strive to "reach" their membership in new ways and respond to new demands and interests of students. The social/cultural and commercial services aspects must not be ignored. In a few colleges political activities and discussion are still discriminated against, although this situation is much better than ten years ago. Student unions should regard the sponsorship of political clubs and societies as a vital part of their activities—and the education of their membership.

*3. Disputes* have been shown to be one of the most important means of unions making progress on democratically decided policies. There is a considerable need for the NUS to assist disputes more effectively in future. This must take several forms—mobilisation of the membership, tactical and legal assistance and, where appropriate, material support. It is unfortunate that after the Polytechnic of North London dispute in 1972 no permanent arrangements were set up to ensure that unions in severe difficulty could be given financial or material assistance. Despite the unwillingness of some to contribute to a central fund it is necessary if the NUS is to be fully effective. NUS reserves are too small for them to be a satisfactory source—without seriously weakening the Union. The NUS could also benefit substantially by producing pamphlets which seek to record and learn from the experience of disputes.

4. *Democratisation* as a trend in student unions needs to be further developed. Student union officers must regard students being involved in the running of their union as a principle of the highest order. It is often "easier" to avoid participation. Student unions are only as strong as their members want them to be or are allowed to make them. This means a style of leadership which will raise the issues that stimulate or oblige students to be involved. It means good organisation and attractive publicity material, and campaigns and militant action, for these can generate a higher level of membership support. Those unions, e.g., at the Universities of Glasgow and St. Andrews, which still seek to involve the mass membership only in the election of the council and office bearers need to institute general meetings as either the governing body or as a crucial part in the decision making process. Contrary to what is often argued on the left, general meetings are not the *only* means of democratic decision making. In multisite institutions or very large colleges general meetings can under some circumstances prevent students participating, due to the absence of appropriately sized meeting facilities, geographical and social dispersion of the students and complex procedures which may cause all but the most committed to be disinterested. Hall meetings, faculty and departmental meetings, site meetings, representative committees and councils should all be utilised. Yet a balance has to be obtained, for if the decision making is too complicated it will either enable important decisions to be easily ignored or not taken at all or produce confusion amongst the students. The objectives of union government should be membership involvement and facility of decision making.

5. *Educational activities* must be extended. There is a tendency amongst students to regard the curriculum as sacrosanct. Student unions should initiate activity in this area, setting up groups of students to criticise courses and the premises on which they are based. It is very important, as it is with student representation, that the union as opposed

to *ad hoc* groups, takes the lead. It is only the union that is able to co-ordinate effectively and generalise with authority on experience gained.

6. *Political activities* are the most contentious that unions can undertake. A small minority of students think that student unions and the NUS should play no part in politics; an equal number by implication assert that student unions should be almost entirely political organisations. Because this can be one of the more difficult areas, it is imperative that democratic practices are scrupulously adhered to. Student unions must undertake solidarity actions with students elsewhere in this country and abroad (particularly in those countries where fascism has banned and curtailed student organisations). In expressing this solidarity it is impossible and undesirable that it be restricted to students alone. Students have found that if their own interests are to be effectively catered for wider alliances and political activities have to be undertaken. Conservatives object to the adoption of political positions, thinking that students should "get on with their own business". It should be regarded as a responsibility for students to consider political issues in their own and wider interests. Not only are political questions in practice inseparable from student and educational issues, but morally students should not seek to isolate themselves or set themselves above political matters. The positions adopted by the NUS are extremely important as a leadership and in setting a framework. As important as the specific policies adopted on Southern Africa, Ireland, Vietnam, Chile, etc., is the political awareness which pervades all the policies and actions of the Union, to its benefit. This situation must continue. Certainly the Union would be strengthened by the development of a position on European peace and security and the Common Market.

Two larger questions are often raised: the attitude of the student movement and the Labour Party and whether the Union should adopt an overall anti-imperialist position. Both are far-reaching in scope and qualitatively different from anything that has been decided so far—for the NUS constitution has always debarred political commitments of such magnitude. Certainly the NUS's 1970 decision in principle to seek affiliation to the TUC raises by implication the question of Labour Party affiliation for the majority of trade unions are affiliated to the

Labour Party. The accepted practice in the trade union world is that individuals can opt out of the political levy when paying their union subscriptions. As students do not pay union subscriptions in the same way, the practice could not be used. The only way it could be done is for the NUS to affiliate to the Labour Party at an agreed *per capita* rate (this would have to be at a lower rate than the trade unions because of the lower level of NUS subscriptions). Given that the membership of NUS is corporate rather than individual student unions could decide to opt out of the political levy. Alternatively NUS could reimburse the political levy to any student seeking to opt out. As with the TUC some special agreement would need to be worked out.

Assuming a heightening of class struggle in the years ahead the possibilities of wider student political involvement will become more important and Labour Party affiliation might be seen as one way of achieving this. An absolute prerequisite for any such decision being taken is a higher level of political discussion and commitment in the student movement. There is a tendency in the NUS sometimes to take decisions lightly. With one of this order, frivolous treatment would discredit, even divide the Union. Every means of involving the membership in the taking of this decision would have to be employed. Regardless of any conclusion to this issue there is a need for the NUS and student unions to intervene in elections to secure the support of candidates on matters of concern to students.

Regarding the overall anti-imperialist position it is equally essential that full democratic debate and discussion takes place as a precondition to any decision. Political commitment undertaken by the NUS or student unions is of little value if it is simply seen by the activists or leadership as politically correct. Unless the membership is able to see the value of this kind of commitment, in terms of the strength and unity of the student movement and the problems they face, there is little point. So the Union will be devalued and its political commitment seen as little more than meaningless posturing. It could be the Achilles heel of the left. On it can be the area of activity which strengthens the NUS and gives it perspective and purpose.

7. *The trade unions* are perhaps the most important area of future development. In 1970 the NUS adopted a full resolution setting out its intention of solidarity with the Labour movement and its desire to co-

operate on issues of joint interest. Since that time local unions and the NUS have proceeded to build a number of relations with the trade union movement.

Students need to become members of trade unions on leaving college. Associate schemes of membership for students as operated by the NUT and ASTMS are a great assistance in this. Bilateral relations and agreements need to be established, as they have been with TASS, between NUS and individual trade unions in order to deal with matters of mutual concern, e.g., NUPE for hall fees and catering charges and NUPE/COHSE for health service students. Multilateral relations with groups of trade unions and the TUC are needed on issues like industrial training, day release and vacation work. Part-time students need to have their interests catered for by student unions and trade unions in co-operation. Student unions need the support of the trade union movement in many of the activities that they undertake locally, and membership of trades councils is very important for this. Trade union representatives on boards of governors need to be briefed on the internal matters so that they will be able to assist the students. Unity is necessary on broad political issues where students and trade unions have developed similar policy, e.g., Vietnam, Chile and apartheid. These and many other links need to be consolidated and developed locally and nationally. Much of this work may appear tiresome and detailed to some student activists, but there is much more to the achievement of worker-student solidarity than the mass mobilisation of students in support of this or that strike or dispute. Mass mobilisation and picketing is essential, but we will be deluding ourselves if we think them sufficient. A network of links between students and trade unionists, organisationally and individually, locally and nationally must be built up. It must be seen both as student self-interest and as a matter of wider social significance. Only if this is done will students be able to be of real assistance to the working class in the struggle for socialism. If it is not done the problems that so sharply appeared in 1968 will recur.

To these ends the NUS needs to establish organisational and even constitutional links with individual trade unions. What of the TUC? The NUS stands for affiliation, but there are considerable constitutional and political difficulties in the way at the present time. To the TUC the NUS is much the same as a tenants' association, a claimants union or an Old Age Pensioners association—none of which can affiliate to the

TUC. NUS might approach the TUC definition of a trade union if students received wages rather than grants. The TUC could alter its rules and constitution to allow the NUS and organisations like it to affiliate. Alternatively, and more realistically, the TUC and the NUS could come to some special agreement about their relationship. It would be wrong for the NUS to press the affiliation issue at the present time, since the General Council would be obliged to turn down an application. No doubt the right wing in the trade unions would like to see the path of unity between students and the Labour movement set back. The political basis for affiliation must first of all exist. The developments of the last three years need to be extended considerably before affiliation can become a question for realistic discussion.

What, then, is the perspective for the National Union of Students?

The Union has in four or five years developed very rapidly. It is the only organisation capable of leading the student body and providing the necessary democratic and organisational framework to service it. Its legitimacy, in this respect so widely challenged previously, is now unchallenged. How secure is this? This could be answered by saying that the National Union has existed for 53 years and it will in all likelihood continue for many more. Yet the NUS has a certain fragility. It rests on the commitment of student unions and their members. Its leaderships are invariably loose coalitions and its conferences racked by fierce controversy. Sectional and sectarian pressures are strong. It holds together because of a wide recognition of its importance in the student world, its record on issues like grants, its services and excellent casework, and its ability to lead and represent.

Nevertheless, prolonged conflict, protracted leadership crises and declining morale in the organisation could damage the credibility of the Union and lay the basis for a split.

The NUS has increased its strength relative to the constituent unions in recent years. There is a greater measure of centralisation than existed previously. A larger proportion of student union subscription income is now paid to NUS. In consequence, a wider range of services is provided. More publications are produced (often seeking to reach the individual student directly). An excellent legal advice service is offered. More conferences and other events are organised.

Some have suggested that the NUS and student unions should become more centralised and less federal. This might result in greater cohesion and discipline but it is unlikely that it would command support from students. The marked element of decentralisation in the NUS and the autonomy of student unions with respect to the NUS is suited to the student movement. The degree to which the NUS can increase its revenue and therefore its services to, and prestige in the student movement, must depend upon its record. In the end the strength of the NUS rests on democracy, the ability to change in response to membership needs.

Since the old right-wing Labour leadership in the NUS was defeated there have been only two alternatives. Either there is a Broad Left leadership composed of militants, radicals, communists and socialists; or more diverse elements, Trotskyists, independents, careerist social democrats, will assume leadership. Because these would not be able to form a cohesive, powerful leadership the alternative would in fact be the Tories outside or inside the Union. Yet the Tories do not have the policies or the mass support to form a credible NUS leadership. So for them to be effective in a mass way the NUS would have to be far less significant than it is now. It is possible that the Tories and various ultra-left groupings between them (albeit in conflict) could have hegemony over the student movement. The Broad Left has existed as a loose coalition for many years. Because of the problems of ultra-leftism and opportunism that arose in 1973–4 it constituted itself on a more formal basis. Regular conferences are now held and a journal has been started. Informality and irregular caucuses are not sufficient any more. A number of problems are facing it. First, the record and practice of the Labour Party in the student movement. Many, many students are non-sectarian, Labour-voting socialists. It is imperative that these are represented in the Broad Left alliance on a permanent basis. Second is the problem of approach. There is a tendency to be preoccupied with factionalism. But the NUS is not a collection of factions with the Broad Left the largest of many. It is a Union and a mass movement.

The present leadership of the Union is mixed in character. There is a Broad Left majority, and an ultra-left minority, with the President trying to balance one against the other. The problem with politics of this kind is that it opens the way to the right. Factionalism goes hand in hand with opportunism and the FCS can pose as the representative body (" the NUS is a bear garden of lefties fighting each other") or can more effectively mount a challenge for the leadership.

In order to avoid these problems experience indicates that the Broad Left should bear the following points in mind. I pose them as pitfalls to be avoided:

1. *Tactical fetishism.* At various times in the recent history of the student movement there has been a tendency to use particular forms of action in a repetitive and unimaginative way. Lobbies, occupations and rent strikes can be over-used—in conditions where they no longer have the support of the mass membership. Behind this is an ability to see policy and politics in a balanced and clear relationship to strategy and tactics. Policy and politics are the principal and ultimate objectives. A strategy is a plan for securing a successful outcome of a campaign or local dispute. Tactics are particular actions undertaken in the strategic context. Tactical flexibility in the context of an unwavering strategic line is the rule. The most militant tactics are not always objectively the best ones.

2. *Opportunism* is to put the short-term advantage of the group or individual in front of the overall strategic or policy objectives of the movement. Right opportunism is an unprincipled move towards respectability, mass inactivity and old style pressure-group politics. Left opportunism is the politics of "revolutionary" posturing and phrase-mongering. Both are equally damaging. A common form of opportunism is where the individual representative either consciously or by default (in the absence of a defined political position) places the advancement of his own position first and other interests second. The damage this does is normally to undermine unity and the strength of the movement. It diverts politics in the direction of the success or failure of the individual and generates a cynicism in the leadership. All forms of opportunism lead to disorientation of the movement.

3. *Sectarianism.* The intervention of Trotskyist groupings in the last three years has made the correct handling of sectarianism a very important issue. Sectarianism means the importation of the methods and practice of the small, detached group or sect into the totally different context of the mass movement. It places the needs of the sect above the needs of the unity of the mass movement. The wrong way of

handling it is to respond in sectarian terms. To play the sectarian game is to concede half their case.

The Broad Left must always put the needs of the mass movement first. This means that all but tactical agreement with the sectarians is impossible—and these on rare occasions. At the same time, ultra-left views are not uncommon in the student world. They represent an immature phase and with a maturing of the movement, argument and polemic, many will be won over. Yet sectarianism can be intoxicating to the politically inexperienced activist. It can be the Achilles heel of the student left.

4. *Rightism.* Some characterise the concern to build up the unity and strength of the mass movement as "lowest common denominator politics". It is only so to those who see an importance in preserving a revolutionary purity divorced from the real world. Yet strategies and tactics that underestimate or play down the potential of the mass movement must be avoided. A top-down approach, the view that the membership must be *told* what to do—in simple, small doses— undermines democratic and participatory possibilities. Routinism and administration must never relegate politics and policy to a subordinate position.

5. *Leadership.* A leadership must not be either too far in front or tail behind the movement. To pose too modest demands can weaken the movement. The posing of unrealistic and very advanced demands must be avoided—it is quite wrong to invite people to sign a false prospectus, even if it is designed to "expose the contradictions" or "lead to greater consciousness". The objectives of a campaign must be able to be seen as attainable by the methods used—or to have a good chance of so doing. Any leadership must scrupulously adhere to democratic principles both within itself and in relation to the mass movement and membership. Leadership is about being told what to do as much as it is about taking a lead within the context of democratically decided policy. A leadership, in the NUS context, must put three principles first—a belief in the actual and potential strength of the Union; a principled commitment to democratic practice and the realisation of the importance of the mass movement as a whole and its unity.

6. *International matters.* Certain aspects of the international position of the Union have always been very sensitive. Experience shows that the extension of fraternal relations with Unions in the socialist countries will not proceed automatically or smoothly. International matters can unite, they can divide and weaken. Sloppy tactics and inadequate regard for democratic practice can lead to failure and ignominious and damaging defeat. I hold that at some point in the future the NUS will need to rejoin the IUS in order to strengthen the unity of the international student movement. But on no account must decisions on this matter be taken without the fullest consultation and opportunity for enquiry on the memberships' part. Lack of full democratic regard will render decisions suspect and perhaps only temporary.

7. *Anti-communism and anti-sovietism.* This is the most dangerous weapon of the ruling class and right wing generally. Cold war lies about "orders from the Kremlin", "communist control", etc., though increasingly shopsoiled, still exert a poisonous effect. Ultra-leftists and careerists, for totally opportunist reasons, are prepared to connive with them. Anti-communism must be fought unremittingly. Its purpose is to weaken and divide the movement. This does not mean that non-communist members of the Broad Left have to behave as apologists for the Communist Party. Differences must be handled in a proper fraternal manner. Communists must for their part ensure that they do not give credence to anti-communism. There is a clear borderline between anti-communism and anti-sovietism on the one hand and proper fraternal discussion and justified criticism of elected officers who are communists on the other. None should forget that anti-communism is still prevalent in our society.

8. *Education and study* are as necessary to the mass movement as they are to the individual. Activists should adopt a historical attitude, for unless the historical determinants of a situation are understood they will not be able to orientate properly in it, still less put forward the best demands and policies for the future. Lenin's advice to Young Communists in 1920 is still timely: "We must not take from the old school the system under which the head of the young man or woman was overburdened with an extraordinary amount of 'knowledge', nine-tenths of which was useless, and the remainder distorted: but this does

not mean that we can limit ourselves only to communist conclusions and learn only communist slogans. You will not establish socialism that way. You will become communists only when you have enriched your minds with the knowledge of all the wealth which humanity has created."

9. The importance of *organisation* is often overlooked in the student movement. It is assumed that because something is agreed, exhortation will make it happen. Petty bourgeois and individualistic fears about bureaucracy and organisation solve no problems and implement no mandates. "Some think that it is sufficient to draw up a correct line, proclaim it from the housetops, state it in the form of general theses and resolutions, and take a vote and carry it unanimously for victory to come of itself, spontaneously, as it were. Only incorrigible red-tapists and bureaucrats can think so. . . . Furthermore, after the correct political line has been laid down, organisational work decides everything, including the fate of the political line itself, its success or failure. . . . Bureaucracy and red tape in the administrative apparatus; idle chatter about 'leadership in general' instead of real and concrete leadership; lack of personal responsibility in work; the absence of a systematic check upon the fulfilment of decisions; fear of self-criticism—these are the sources of our difficulties." That was written by Stalin in 1934. Though the context was very different all the points have much validity for all involved in the Broad Left. Politics and policy must come first, but organisational weaknesses remain major problems facing the Broad Left.

This book has sought to give a background to and make an assessment of the contemporary student movement. The first two chapters concentrated on the material and institutional/educational circumstances in which students find themselves. Severe educational expenditure cuts which the present Labour Government shows no signs of reversing will very seriously affect all aspects of higher and further education. The prevention or at least the amelioration of the effects of these cuts is one of the major tasks facing the student movement.

Chapters 3 and 4 looked at the history of student organisations in Britain and how they have changed in recent years: The magnitude of this change, in reality and potential, is substantial. The bitter, divisive legacy of the cold war has been largely overcome and student unions and NUS have emerged stronger from the experience. Yet the very shortness of student generations means that students in 1974–5 know little or nothing of the situation a few years ago. Each new intake of students has to learn and relearn the lessons of the past in new circumstances. Because of this and the "action now" approach immanent in the student body, mistakes once made can be repeated. This aspect of the student world can produce a refreshing and dynamic vitality or a boring repetitiveness. Unions and the NUS have had and will have a major role to play here to synthesise the experience and aspirations of the student body into coherent policies, themselves to be organised around and implemented. Without them, as international comparison shows, the student movement would be volatile, formless and somewhat ineffective.

Chapter 5 examined the character of the student movement in a wider social and political context. Whilst in my view insecure employment and career prospects of students are the most potent factors (themselves the product of the crisis of British capitalism), the student body reflects political and social instability in a unique way. The present political situation in Britain has both considerable need and potential for social change. The acceleration of détente, the advance of national liberation and of the socialist countries, and the overall weakening of the position of the imperialist countries (particularly Britain), are a challenge to the working-class and progressive movement. Trade union militancy and consciousness is on the upswing, as is the prestige of the left in the Labour movement. Yet, at the same time there are many difficulties—the divisiveness of racialism, the opportunist and defeatist leadership of the Labour Party, and the strength and guile of the British ruling class. The economic and political indicators are that class struggle and other social conflicts and tensions will increase. In these circumstances I believe that the student movement cannot and will not stand idly by. It must fight for its own interests and alongside the working class for more radical social changes. Whilst students are no longer the strikebreakers and blacklegs of 1926 and a start has been made in developing unity between students and the trade unions, it would be sheer naïveté to imagine that the problem at a mass level has had more than an "airing". Until a mass student movement assumes more concrete, permanent and political forms in the context of a wider political alliance around the working class, then what Lenin called "intellectual insipidness" and "sentimental love of the people" or their more modern form, vanguardism, are likely to re-emerge as negative factors.

Ultimately, it is socialism created by the revolutionary overthrow of capitalism by the working class and its allies which can provide the conditions for the full satisfaction of student demands and the emancipation of all the people. There is no higher vocation than to try to bring this objective nearer. For the student body and its leadership this means the need to sustain a powerful mass movement, organised, strongly influenced by socialist ideas and committed in struggle to the side of the working class.

## CHARTER OF STUDENT RIGHTS AND RESPONSIBILITIES, 1940

600 students gathered at the British Student Congress at Leeds,

DEEPLY CONSCIOUS of the inequality, the poverty and the destruction of human life and values which characterise our society,

BELIEVING that the Universities, Colleges and Training Colleges of Great Britain have an indispensable part to play in the advance towards a new, peaceful and just society,

AWARE that they are not at present fully playing that part,

REALISING that British students have the responsibility of ensuring that the knowledge and culture of the universities are used in the interests of the people as a whole, of ensuring that university education is not a privilege of a class, and of working with all sections of the people to this end,

CONFIDENT that the students of Britain will contribute their share to the efforts of progressive humanity, inside and outside the universities, to secure peace and justice for all peoples,

FIRMLY convinced that freedom, liberty and democracy within the universities and colleges are essential if they are to implement their responsibilities towards the community,

and having heard evidence of recent encroachments upon student liberties:

WARN the students of Britain of the danger of further attacks,

AND CALL UPON THEM to work in unity and with all their strength for this Charter of Student Rights:

### THE CHARTER

THE RIGHT to the free expression of opinion by speech and Press.

THE RIGHT to organise meetings, discussion and study on all subjects within the university and college precincts.

THE RIGHT to participate to the full in all activities outside the universities, and to collaborate with extra-university organisations.

THE RIGHT to share in the government and administration of the universities.

Given these rights,

WE PLEDGE ourselves to fulfil our responsibilities to the community,

AND CALL on all students to defend them by their united action, and all sections of the British People, for their support.

## A RADICAL STUDENT ALLIANCE

We have set out here what we believe to be a programme necessary for the interests of students, for the removal of barriers to a full and democratic education, and for the greatest contribution of students to society and social progress. We invite students' unions, all kinds of student groups and individuals to express their opinions on it, and if they think fit, to associate themselves with our effort.

| | | |
|---|---|---|
| David Adelstein | Allan Jones | Alan Richardson |
| Chris Farrer | David Laing | Terry Lacey |
| Alan Hunt | Malcolm McCallum | Mervyn Saunders |
| Martin Jacques | Adrian Perry | Janet Royle |

### STUDENTS' RIGHTS

1. Students should have the right to complete control over their own unions and funds, without interference, to elect their officers and representatives and determine their own policies.

2. Students should have the right to effective participation in all other decisions that affect them, notably in academic, financial welfare and disciplinary matters.

3. Students should have the right to study free from financial barriers. This requires full and adequate maintenance, without means test, for everyone in full time education over school leaving age.

### EDUCATION

4. Education must be classless, integrated (not "tripartite" or "binary") and comprehensive at all levels. Adequate remuneration to secure a sufficient supply of teaching staff must not be delayed by the wage freeze, or incomes policy.

5. Undemocratic pressures on college government must be resisted; vigilance is needed in respect of the influence of industry on education

and research; college authorities should be more democratically composed to include representatives of students, non-professorial staff and trade unions.

## STUDENTS & SOCIETY

6. Students as an organised body must be able to take collective action on matters of general social concern when there is a substantial consensus of student opinion, for example, action in opposition to racialism wherever it occurs and for the eradication of its causes in society.

7. There should be active co-operation with students in other countries, and in particular solidarity with those who are victims of oppression.

## STUDENTS' AIMS AND ORGANISATIONS

8. Lack of militancy and perspective have so far prevented student organisations from achieving these aims. But no organisation is entitled by virtue of its own constitution to represent students. If an organisation is to speak for students it must be heard to speak for them, or in default others will. We propose to work through and outside existing organisations for the development of a democratic and active student movement, based on strong local and area unions and organisations, autonomous and democratic.

9. Students need national unions closer to their members by virtue of frequent participation and involvement of the membership in making and implementing policy, led by representative leadership rather than self-perpetuating cliques.

10. Student society is not a closed one and the successful pursuit of these aims makes necessary co-operation with educational and other trade unions and professional associations, locally and nationally, for common aims.

Published by Radical Student Alliance, c/o Youth Office,
36, Smith Sq., London S.W.1.

## RSSF—MANIFESTO FOR A
## POLITICAL PROGRAMME, 1968

The Revolutionary Socialist Students Federation:

Commits itself to the revolutionary overthrow of capitalism and imperialism and its replacement by workers' power, and bases itself on the recognition that the only social class in industrial countries capable of making the revolution is the working class.

Opposes all forms of discrimination and will lend its support to any group engaged in progressive struggle against such discrimination.

Commits itself on principle to all anti-imperialist, anti-capitalist and anti-fascist struggles and resolutely opposes all forms of capitalist domination and class collaboration.

Will lend its support to any group of workers or tenants in struggles against the wage freeze and price and rent increases.

Constitutes itself as an extra-parliamentary opposition because its aims cannot be achieved through parliamentary means.

Extends to all left students and organisations the invitation to co-operate with it in supporting and organising for its aims, and extends fraternal greetings to organisations abroad already doing so.

Recognises that the trend of modern capitalism to the increasing integration of manual and mental labour, of intellectual and productive work, makes the intellectual element increasingly crucial to the development of the economy and society and that this productive force comes into sharpening conflict with the institutional nature of capitalism. The growing revolutionary movement of students in all advanced capitalist countries is a product of this. To organise this vital sector as a revolutionary ally of the proletariat and as an integral part of the building of a new revolutionary movement, RSSF resolutely opposes ruling-class control of education and determines to struggle for an education system involving comprehensive higher education, the abolition of the binary system, public schools and grammar schools, the transformation of this sector requires the generation of a revolutionary socialist culture.

Believes that existing political parties and trade unions cannot either structurally or politically sustain revolutionary socialist programmes. It affirms that it is neither meaningful nor valuable to attempt to capture these organisations. While retaining support for their defensive struggles, it believes that new, participatory mass-based organisations are required to overthrow capitalism.

Believes that students will play a part in the building of such organisations and in the linking of struggles of existing militant groups. It sees its particular role as developing socialist consciousness among youth.

Believes that the institutions of higher education are a comparatively weak link in British capitalism, and that the ruling class' field of action can be severely restricted by correctly waged struggles for student control and universities of revolutionary criticism.

RSSF will build red bases in our colleges and universities by fighting for the following Action Programme:

ALL POWER TO THE GENERAL ASSEMBLY OF STUDENTS, STAFF AND WORKERS—ONE MAN ONE VOTE ON THE CAMPUS.

**Abolition of all exams and grading.**

**Full democracy in access to higher education.**

**An end to bourgeois ideology—masquerading as education— in courses and lectures.**

**Abolition of all inequality between institutions of higher education—against hierarchy and privilege.**

**Break the authority of union bureaucracies and institute mass democracy.**

*ADOPTED by 2nd RSSF conference—London November 10 1968*

## THE NATURE OF STUDENT UNIONS

Student unions now have a wider range of functions. They are accordingly stronger. They:

1. Provide essential social and cultural facilities for students. Societies existing under the umbrella of the union and receiving grant from it are very wide ranging. Entertainments and sporting activities provide an essential corporate element to college existence.
2. Assist the individual student in his day-to-day difficulties in college. The casework may be of a counselling type or involve taking up a grievance with the college authorities. The union is on the student's side.
3. Provide an essential exercise in democratic government and participation. Students with an autonomous union are involved in an experience which is profoundly educative. They are deciding what they wish to do. This is an essential complement to the formal education provided by the college.
4. Provide services of commercial benefit to the individual student. Stationery, beer, entertainment and snacks are the most common in this category. The NUS caters for travel and insurance in particular.
5. Provide a channel or communication between the student body and the college authority.
6. Are a framework within which the student representation in college government can be properly co-ordinated and led.
7. Are a union which will defend and advance, i.e. trade union fashion, the interests of students *vis-à-vis* the college authority, LEA or the Government.
8. Provide an opportunity for wider debate, discussion and action on matters of concern to others as well as students.

All these activities are interrelated. It is particularly important for unions to engender a social and community atmosphere if they are to fulfil their more political responsibilities.

A fundamental principle of student unions is that they have automatic membership (sometimes called compulsory membership). This has been fought for over many years and still has not been conceded in some areas.

Prior to 1962 LEA's paid student union fees on a voluntary basis. In this year the Standing Advisory Committee on student grants, the body which in that year reviewed the level of student grants, recommended that union fees should be met as a tuition cost. They held, as the NUS had represented to them, that student unions were an essential component in a wider education. The DES letter of December 3rd, 1962, implemented the principle and laid down that for colleges of education payment should be up to £2·50 *per capita*. In turn this figure was raised to £3 for colleges of education and technical colleges. It has stayed at the same level since.

Automatic membership means that so long as the student is registered at the college for a course he is automatically a member of the union. He has no choice about this membership, but he is not obliged to do anything by the union or any part of it. This provides the opportunity of involvement, since the facilities, societies, journals etc., are financed by the subscription income. It establishes a student body, an idea and a reality that the overwhelming majority of students have always desired. Some assert that "compulsory" membership is an encroachment on the freedom of the individual, and that it is like the closed shop. It is not the same as the closed shop. The situation in colleges is not the same as the shop floor. It resembles more the principle of citizenship of the older Scottish universities and the notion in universities generally that students and staff alike are members of an academic community.

Tuition costs or fees are part of the recurrent expenditure of the college or university. They are not the only source of recurrent income, but they are historically very important, as they date from the time when all students were fee-paying (from their own sources) and higher education was largely private, like the public schools. When a student is accepted on to a course of full-time higher education he will in nearly every case receive a maintenance grant. In so doing the tuition fees will also be paid on his behalf. If the student has parents on a relatively high income then the parents or the student will be expected to pay for maintenance (minus a £50 minimum grant) and the tuition fees. The college authority on receipt of the tuition fees has to pay over to the union the subscription income as a lump sum. In theory all institutions of higher education can fix their own level of tuition fees, though in practice this is not so. College authorities are, however, able to decide the level of student union income (in the case of most public sector institutions this power basically lies with the LEA). The level of union fee depends on whether the institution is a university or not, the amount of advanced course work and the numbers of full-time students. In the case of students on courses which do not command mandatory awards, the LEA's may or may not pay union fees. Here levels of subscription are very variable and the union can in this situation expect payment by individual students from their own pockets. Some technical and further education colleges still operate on this voluntary membership basis. These unions resemble clubs more than unions. The voluntary practice is declining.

Automatic union membership confers both advantages and disadvantages. The union has a guaranteed source of income and membership. Accordingly, it is much easier to organise and plan activities. On the other hand, the money comes through the college authority which may lead the latter to think that it can interfere with the process of payment or use improper political pressure. Such action is illegal and cannot be done unless the union has acted *ultra vires* its constitution. More important, it establishes the union as an integral part of the college, though integral does not mean integrated. Unions have sought and obtained recognition as the means of communication between authority and students. Recognition in the charter and statutes or instrument and articles of government and the receipt of funds in the manner described gives the college authority some power, normally notional or theoretical, over the content of student union constitutions. They have to be approved by the college authority as a precondition for the receipt of funds. Approval could mean that the college would choose to rewrite the constitution (though if a college did so the courts would probably say that they were acting unreasonably—and the students would rightly protest). Usually it means ratification, which in most cases is a formality. It is rare for college authorities to refer back, still less to disallow constitutional amendments submitted by student unions. Some authorities and student unions have arrangements whereby all but the most important clauses can be amended without recourse to the governors. Once approved, the union is autonomous within its constitution and the laws of the land. The danger of interference by college authorities is most likely in financial matters where the annual accounts of the union by convention are approved (ratified) by the college. This is a necessity if the union is seeking a subscription increase. In the last analysis the relationship of the student union and college authority is political rather than constitutional or legal. It is generally not in the interest of college authorities to provoke autonomy disputes with the union as this is always a very sensitive issue to the students. In practice, therefore, student unions have a substantial area of *de facto* autonomy.

# INDEX

Academic freedom, 12, 93, 137, 161
Academic Freedom and the Law Report, 66
Access to higher education (*see also* GCE's), 20–5, 128–33
  central registry, 130
  counselling, 130
  course rigidity, 131
  departmentalism and hierarchy, 130–2
  entrance requirements, 131
  mature students, 129
  variations between universities, 129
Adams, Sir Walter, 86
Adelstein, David, 92, 163
Alexander, Sir William, 58
Arblaster, Anthony, 12
Ashby, Eric and Anderson, Mary, 11, 73, 77, 78
Association of Scientific Managerial and Scientific Staffs, 152
Association of Teachers in Technical Institutions, 34, 144
Association of University Teachers, 78
Aston University, 129
Atkinson, Dick, 72, 93

Barnett, Anthony, 113, 114
Barr, Alan, 142
B.Ed. degree, 36, 37, 38, 129
Beard, Ruth, 12
Binary system, 25–30, 144 (*see also* Comprehensive post-school education)
Birkbeck College, 26, 129
Birmingham University, 48, 72, 76, 93, 106, 129, 141
Blackburn, Robin, 72, 93
Bradford University, 129
Brighton College of Education, 106
British Universities Congress, 77

British Youth Peace Assembly, 79
Broad Left, 87, 104, 106, 109, 154, 155–8
Brosan, George, 28
Brunel University, 30, 129
Burnham Further Education Report, 132
Butterworth, Jack, 46
Brynmor-Jones Report (audio-visual aids), 126

Caine, Sir Sydney, 11, 77
Cambridge University, 9, 20, 27, 43, 134
  Economics Faculty dispute, 93
  origins of student unions, 73–7
  suicide rates, 60
Campaign for Nuclear Disarmament, 85, 107
Carter, Charles, 12
Catering boycotts, 92
Central Intelligence Agency, 84, 85, 91, 94
Chamberlain, Neville, 80
Chamberlain, Sir Joseph, 48
Chambers, Sir Paul, 47
City and Guilds London Institute courses, 54
City University, 129
Clarendon Commission, 74
Cohn-Bendit, Daniel, 11
Colleges of Advanced Technology, 17, 25, 33, 35, 43, 48
Committee of Polytechnic Directors, 51
Committee of Vice-Chancellors and Principals, 11, 20
Communist Party of Great Britain, 13, 86, 103–7, 157
Communist University of London, 106, 141
Comprehensive post-school education (*see also* Binary system)

Comprehensive post-school education—*cont.*
institutional autonomy, 146
institutional reorganisations, 145
RSA charter, 163
age group, 16–18, 144–5
Confederation of British Industry, 48
Conféderation Général du Travail, 90
Confederation of Health Service Employees, 152
Conféderation Internationale des Étudiants, 77
Conservative Party (Federation of Conservative Students), 115–17, 154
Cook, Dave, 106
Council for Further and Higher Education, 144, 145, 146
Council for National Academic Awards, 24, 38, 45, 68
Craig, David, 72, 93
Cronkite, Walter, 90
Crosland, C. A. R., 25, 27, 28, 87, 143
Crouch, Colin, 11, 12
Crowther Report (15–18), 21
Curriculum, 71–2, 80
disputes, 93
ideology, 140–1
objectives, 138–41
Student Community Action, 142–3
student unions, 149–50

Dainton Report (flow of candidates in science and technology into h.e.), 71
Defence contracts, 47
Department of Education and Science (*see also* Education a framework for expansion; Weaver, Toby; and chapter 1 generally)
Circular 7/70, 32
Circular 7/71, 41
Design Technician Certificate, 41
Diploma in Art and Design, 39, 40, 41
Diploma in Higher Education, 38, 48, 51, 127

Donaldson, Lex, 35
Durham University, 74
Dutschke, Rudi, 90

Edinburgh University, 75
Education Act 1944, 25, 62, 98
Education a framework for expansion, 19, 24, 31, 38, 45, 50–2, 127
Educational options, 70
course units, 70–1
curriculum, 139
deferred entry, 139–40
Educational Planning Paper, 2, 19, 24
Essex University, 92

Family Law Reform Act, 99
Farrer, Chris, 163
Fawthrop, Tom, 67, 124
Fernbach, David, 113, 115
Finnish National Union of Students (SYL), 134
Fisk, Trevor, 95
Fowler, Gerry, 50
French Communist Party, 111

General Certificate in Education (Ordinary and Advanced levels), 130, 128, 129, 130, 131 (*see also* Access to higher education)
entrance requirements, 41–2, 45, 51, 67, 120
Glasgow University, 149
Graduate unemployment, 61–2, 98
Gretton, John, 12
Grimond Review Body (Birmingham University), 63
Guildford School of Art, 89, 91, 93, 95, 114
Guest Keen and Nettlefolds, 48
Guevara, Che, 89, 115

Hale Report (university teaching methods), 126
Halifax, Lord, 81
Hart Report (Committee on Relations with Junior Members at Oxford University), 64
Heaf, Peter, 105
Heath, Edward, 117

Henniker-Heaton Report (day release), 31
Heriot-Watt University, 76, 129
Heron, Patrick, 42
Higher Education Commission, 144
Higher National Certificate/Higher National Diploma, 30, 120, 129, 131
Higher School Certificate, 130
Hoch, Paul, 11, 89
Hornsey College of Art, 12, 89, 91, 93, 95, 114, 134
Horsbrugh, Florence, 83
House of Commons, Public Expenditure Committee, 25, 144
Hull University, 129
Hunt, Alan, 163
Hunt, Gilbert, 46

Instrument and Articles of Government, 35
International Socialism Group, 88–9
International Student Conference, 82, 85, 94
International Union of Students, 82–3, 84, 85, 104, 157
Institutes of Education, 44

Jacques, Martin, 163
James Committee, Report on teacher education, 37, 41
Joint Working Party Report (Summerson-Coldstream Committee), 40
Jones, Allan, 163

Keele University, 92
Kelsall, Professor, 20
Kidd, Harry, 11
King's College, London, 75
Klug, Brian, 124

Labour Party, 107–10, 144, 150, 151, 154, 159
Labour Party Young Socialists, 108
Lacey, Terry, 163
Laing, David, 163
Lancaster University, 72, 93, 96
Lanchester College of Technology, 45
Layard, Richard, et al., 12

Leeds University, 76, 79, 129, 161
Leicester University, 106
Lenin, V. I., 101, 157, 160
Lewis, Kenneth, MP, 117
Library Association, 27
Liverpool University, 76, 129
London School of Economics, 72, 77, 86, 92, 93, 95, 116

Macadam, Sir Ivison, 78
Madden, Tom, 82
Malleson, Dr. Nicholas, 60
Manchester University, 9, 74, 96, 129
Mandel, Ernest, 110, 111, 112
Marcuse, Herbert, 110, 112
Marischal College, 75
Martin, Geoffrey, 95
Media, 10, 87
and "student revolution", 90, 110
Middlesex Polytechnic, 35
Middleton, Geoffrey, 116
Militant Group, 108–9
Monday Club, 97, 117
Montgomery, Dr. David, 46
Movimento Studentesco, 91
Murray Enquiry (Governance of London University), 63
Macarthy Report, 71
McCallum, Malcolm, 163
McNair Report, 1944, 80

Nagel, Julian, 12
Nairn, Tom, 12, 111
National Association of Labour Student Organisations, 107, 108
National Children's Bureau (from birth to seven), 21
National Diploma in Design, 39
National Federation of Socialist Societies, 107
National Organisation of Labour Students, 108–9
National Union of Public Employees, 152
National Union of Students, 14
as pressure group, 83–4
assessment, 125
binary policy, 25–26, 144
Broad Left, 154
1940 Charter, 79–80, 161–2

National Union of Students—*cont.*
Clause 3, Aims and Objects, 94, 150
Congress, 79, 107
Curriculum, 72
disputes, 92, 95, 148
early years, 78–9
Federation of Conservative Students, 116–17
grants campaigns, 122
grants reviews, 55
International Student Conference, 82
International Students Day, 81–2
International Union of Students, 82–5, 157
Left leadership, 96
Legal Aid Fund, 96
leadership weaknesses, 87, 91
move to left, 94–5
multiple transferable voting, 94
origins, 77
1966 Polytechnics White Paper, 34
perspectives and policies, 13, 118, 146–54
and RSSF, 88
Second World War, 81
Student Community Action, 142–3
student movement, 73
student representation, 62
teaching methods survey, 126, 129
Travel Department, 78, 167
under challenge 1966, 86, 164
National Union of School Students, 147
NUS Travel Ltd., 78
National Union of Teachers, 108, 152
Newcastle University, 77, 129
Newsom Report (Half Our Future), 21
New University of Ulster, 129
New Universities, 43–4
Nicholson, Fergus, 105
Nonington College of Physical Education, 92
North East London Polytechnic, 28

Ordinary National Certificate/ Ordinary National Diploma, 30, 54, 120, 129, 131
Open University, 26, 70, 131
Overseas Students, 87, 121
Overspecialisation (see also curriculum), 71
Oxford University, 9, 20, 27, 43, 134
suicide rates, 60
origins of student unions, 73–5, 77

Perry, Adrian, 163
Pilkington Committee—Technical College Resources, 34
Piper, David Warren, 40
Polytechnic of North London, 62, 148
Polytechnics White Paper, 1966, 31, 34, 146
Porter Butts, 73–4
Powell, Enoch, 99
Prentice, Reg, 50
Proctors, 66

Quattrocchi, Angelo, 12, 111
Queen's University, Belfast, 76
Quinn, Linda, 65, 92

Radical Student Alliance
character, 87–8
dispute with NUS leadership, 94
charter, 163–4
NALSO, 107
origins, 86
student representation, 134
Raison, Timothy, 97
Red bases, 113–15, 166
Regional Advisory Councils (for further education), 145
Rent strikes, 92
Revolutionary Socialist Students Federation
and Communist Party, 104
foundation, 88–9
manifesto, 165–6
and red bases, 114
sectarianism, 92
socialist societies, 107
Rhodes, Frank, 11
Richardson, Alan, 163
Robbins Committee (Report on

Robbins Committee—*cont.*
  Higher Education, 25, 31, 33, 36, 43, 100
  assessment, 14–20
  Communist Party evidence, 103
  housing for students, 57
  NUS evidence, 83–4
Robinson, Eric, 28
Rothschild Report (scientific research), 47
Rowntree, John and Margaret, 110
Royal College of Art—big three, 27
Royle, Janet, 163
Rubin, Jerry, 90
Russell Report (teacher training for further education), 127
Ryle, Anthony, 60

St. Andrew's University, 149
Salford University, 129
Sandwich courses, 48, 70, 123
Saunders, Mervyn, 163
Schools Council—Standing Conference on University Entrance working party, 67
SISTER, 17
Scottish Association of Labour Student Organisations, 107
Scottish Union of Students, 75, 77
Sheffield University, 76, 78, 129
Short, Edward, 67, 97
Simon, Brian, 79
Simpson, Edward, 59
Slack, Jonathan, 140–1
Smith, Leo, 67
Socialist Labour League, 107
Spock, Dr., 97
Stalin, Joseph, 158
Standing Advisory Committee (student awards), 168
Standing Conference of Regional Advisory Councils, 144
Stirling University, 46, 65, 76, 96
  students' association, 92
Strathclyde university, 76
Straw, Jack, 95
Student Assessment
  control of students, 67
  disputes, 93
  examinations, weaknesses of, 67–8

grading, objections, 68–9
  profiles, 124, 131
  suggested policy, 123–6
Student community action, 141–3
Student Co-operative Dwellings, 59
Student counselling, 60–1, 130–1
Student discipline
  campus contract, 66
  disputes, 92
  double discipline, 64
  in *loco parentis*, 63, 64
  rights of fair hearing, representation and appeal, 64
  extent of college regulations, 65–6
  victimisation, 66, 99
Student grants, 28
  declining value, 55, 98, 120
  disincentive to study, 53, 163
  discipline, 57
  first degree courses, 54
  discretionary awards, 119–20
  parental dependence, 54, 119
  pocket money, 56
  postgraduates, 54, 56
  sandwich courses, 56
  sexual discrimination, 55, 120
  suggested policy, 119–23
  vacation grants, 56
  vacation work, 55, 120
Student housing
  expansion of higher education, 57
  Housing Finance Act 1972, 58
  loan financed construction, 57–8
  multioccupation, 58
  regionalisation of intake, 58–9
  self-help methods, 59
  disputes, 92
Student Labour Federation, 83, 107
Student loans, 56–7, 121
Student movement
  definition, 13
  international comparisons, 90–2
  local issues and disputes, 92–4
  NUS, 73, 95–6
  reasons for change, 97–100
  working class, 100–2
Student non-Violent Co-ordinating Committee, 141
Student power, 87–8, 103, 134
Student representation

Student representation—*cont.*
  colleges of education, 38
  different approaches, 133–5
  disputes, 93, 98
  1940 NUS Charter, 162
  RSA charter, 163
  Polytechnic of North London, 62
  proposals for change, 136–8
  shortcomings, 63
Student unions
  automatic membership, 167–9
  autonomy, 92, 96, 99, 114, 147, 163, 169
  class struggle, 103
  curriculum, 149–50
  debating unions, 73–5
  cultural activities, 148
  democratic nature, 105, 167
  fees, 27, 147
  further education, 32, 147
  general meetings, 95, 106, 149
  Junior Common Rooms, 44
  NUS, 154
  NUS subscriptions, 153
  origins, 73–7
  perspectives and policies, 146–54
  registrar, 117
  RSSF, 88, 114
  Scotland, 75–6, 149
  Student Representative Councils, 73–7
  trade unions, 102–3, 105, 167, 168
Student vanguardism (*see also* red bases), 88, 104, 110–12
Student wages, 119, 122–3
Students for a Democratic Society (SDS), 91, 110
Students for a Labour Victory, 107–8
Surrey University, 37, 129
Sussex University, 129

Teaching methods
  teaching and research, 126
  lectures, 126–7
  lecturer training, 127–8
  student participation, 128

TASS (AUEW staff section), 152
Technical Education (1956 White Paper), 25, 33, 146
Thatcher, Margaret, 37, 50
Thompson, Edward, et al., 12
Tinckham, Linda, 35
Toynbee, Philip, 97
Trades Union Congress
  and NUS, 105
  and NUT, 108
  NUS affiliation, 150–1, 152–3
Trade union and labour movement, 80, 101, 118, 136, 148, 150, 151–3, 159
Tribune Group, 108
Triesman, David, 113

Union National des Etudiants Français (UNEF), 91
United States National Student Association, 84, 91, 94
Universities Central Council on Admissions, 130
Universities (Scotland) Act, 75
University College, Cardiff, 129
University College, London, 75
University College, Rhodesia, 86
University College, Swansea, 96, 129
University Grants Committee, 26, 57, 61, 145
University of Wales Institute of Science and Technology, 129

Vansittart, Lord, 81
Verband Deutscher Studenten (VDS), 91

Warwick University, 45, 46, 93
Watherston, Peter, 116
Weaver, Toby—Report, 28, 62
Wilby, Peter, 10
Wilson, Harold, 17, 89
Wright, Charles, 67

Zweig, Ferdynand, 9